"Oh, My Glory!

"Oh, My Glory!"

✦

Marion: In A League of Her Own

Denise Rush

iUniverse, Inc.

New York Lincoln Shanghai

"Oh, My Glory!"
Marion: In A League of Her Own

iUniverse books may be ordered through booksellers or by contacting:

iUniverse
2021 Pine Lake Road, Suite 100
Lincoln, NE 68512
www.iuniverse.com
1-800-Authors (1-800-288-4677)

Because of the dynamic nature of the Internet, any Web addresses or links contained in this book may have changed since publication and may no longer be valid.

The views expressed in this work are solely those of the author and do not necessarily reflect the views of the publisher, and the publisher hereby disclaims any responsibility for them.

ISBN: 978-0-595-49459-0 (pbk)
ISBN: 978-0-595-61111-9 (ebk)

Printed in the United States of America

For Our Nana

A woman whose life illuminates in glory—not the fleeting type that is lost on earthly fame and fortune—but the eternally earned glory of love and respect that comes from years of putting others first without ever a thought of self in mind; only praise for those you meet and their talents is on your lips. The time has come, however, for your family to sing your praises.

"Oh, my Glory!"

Marion Rush

Contents

Acknowledgments

Marion Edith Rush is not only the subject matter of this book, but is also the main person I would like to take the opportunity to thank. Without her input during many "interview sessions"/visits and telephone calls, I would not have been able to gather the information needed to make her story come to life. I also wish to thank her for her genuine enthusiasm and the constant confidence she exhibited in my writing ability—more than I have in myself. I also wish to thank her for her efforts and the great pains she took to bring this book to fruition. (She literally did undergo great pains manipulating a tape recorder while recuperating from a broken shoulder in order to dictate the copious questions and answers used as prompts for biographical background.) You are my glory, my heroine!

Along those lines, I could not have done this without the love and support of the love of my life, my husband and best friend, Eddie. He is by far the greatest gift of glory in my prejudicial eyes that Marion has given to the world. After tiring days at work and on weekends and vacations, he would help me transcribe his mother's taped dictations, so that I could literally keep my fingers on the keys instead of pressing the rewind and fast forward buttons. He also was the sounding board who listened to all the first drafts of chapters as they were written. Also, I wish to thank our daughter, Lauren, who helped tremendously with this endeavor by using her computer wizardry and graphic skills to copy and embed pictures into the appropriate spots within text. Scott, our son, also took pictures and helped in this regard. We are so blessed with you both as our children. Thank you all for your patience with me. My parents, Leo and Vee, also listened intently to my writing trials and tribulations, without jealousy or animosity in the fact that I, their daughter, was writing my mother-in-law's biography and not theirs. My family, I love you all dearly.

The "village" of relatives and friends who have helped our heroine, Marion/Nana, also need to receive their accolades: Jim Sr., Jim Jr., Kathy, Kelly, Kara, Pat & Richard, Avis & Don, Cathy & Kenny, Donna & Bill, Junie, Alan & Heather, Billy & Roberta, Fr. Paul Gilbert, and all the others who have helped Marion in her later years deserve much more credit than I, or anyone else, can give them.

A gracious thank you goes out, additionally, to anyone I have inadvertently forgotten to mention.

Also, in regards to some historic information within the book, I would like to thank a very good friend who was invaluable in finding information, the Internet Web site: *Wikipedia*. Whoever these people are who put this together deserve the Pulitzer Prize. Also, I wish to acknowledge *The Boston Herald* for graciously allowing the pictures of a young softball player named Marion Schulze to be included in this biography, as well as the New England Sports Museum in Boston, Massachusetts. (A team photo of the *Boston Olympets* was displayed on exhibit there in 1992 during the debut of the film *A League of Their Own*, honoring the women from New England who played professional baseball and softball during World War II. That photo is included in this book.)

Finally, for all those same women … I know I speak for Marion, when I say: "This one's for you, too!"

Preface

"Oh, my Glory!" Why would anyone want to read a book about an ordinary woman? Why would any woman want to write a book about their mother-in-law?

Well, to answer these two questions, you would have to meet my mother-in-law: Marion Schulze Rush. She may be an ordinary woman, but the lessons that her life teaches are more than extraordinary, and, in my eyes, she is one-in-a-million. Marion is and always was the ultimate team player in life. She is the person you want on your side: she always pulls more than her share of the weight, she never tries to take all the glory, instead letting her teammates bask in its glow, and, most importantly—she never whines or complains about anything, including the aches and pains that have come her way, even the big one that starts with a "C"—*cancer*—colon cancer to be specific. Yet, when Marion stepped up to the plate to face that monstrous opponent, she gave it all she had and she beat him down. Now, she is facing another, CHF (congestive heart failure), and she is, to this very day, struggling and winning this one in extra innings at the age of 90.

On all the clubs and teams in life she has been a member of, she is and always will be the MVP. Now, for those of you not fluent in sportsology, that means most valuable player, or in Marion's case … most valuable person. She is, from my perspective, far and away—*In a League of **Her** Own.*

Now, you may be thinking I'm plagiarizing the title from the movie made famous by Geena Davis, Madonna, and Tom Hanks called *A League of **Their** Own,* but you must understand, however, that the title is just too appropriate and befitting not to use a portion of it to describe my mother-in-law, Marion. Truth be told, she would have been one of the characters portrayed in that movie if fate had not thrown her a different curve ball. In this book, you will discover, that she also would have been "discovered" along with the top women's baseball players of that movie on the team *The Racine Belles* if she had not met my father-in-law, gotten married, had children, and lived the very ordinary yet wonderful life she has to this day. (In the early 1940s, Marion Schulze (a.k.a. Schulzie, or Wo-Wo to her brother Al, played semi-professional softball in the Boston Garden for a team known as *The Olympets* (better known in the days of the pre-feminist era as: *The Pets)* and was offered to go out west and play for the *Racine Belles*. She turned

xiii

it down and, in typical Marion fashion, does not, in any way, shape, or form, regret that decision. She was not upset over this glory lost, for glory is not what she is about. Anyone who meets her knows that fact.

Marion's famous saying that every family member has heard her exclaim in enthusiastic gusto at one time or another is: "Oh my Glory!" As you read this book, you will become keenly aware that she is not—and never has been—one to seek attention and fame. She puts herself last in line for everything and is appreciative of even the smallest gesture. She is selfless. To me, this is the hallmark of true greatness, the mark, I believe, of a saint. My mother-in-law, Marion Rush, is such a person, a genuine gem of a woman who is forever the optimist, upbeat, unassuming, ordinary, and yet extraordinary for all those reasons. She is, and always has been, an uncomplicated woman with just enough naïveté to make her sweetly endearing. In fact, Marion is our family's Norm Crosby, especially when it comes to the medical language. She, like the classic act of that comedian, can twist a phrase to the delight of all within earshot. Yet, she is keenly smart and a whiz with numbers and statistics (especially sports stats). Marion is a woman of character: hard-working, devoted to her family, a doer of good deeds, loyal, and highly competitive; she is a woman who is and always will be *In a League of Her Own*—not a Geena Davis, or Madonna the rock star, that is, but the closest thing to the *real Madonna*, the saintly matriarch and shining star of our family.

—Denise Rush

1

The 'Glory-ous' Fall

She fell with a thud out of the blue—didn't even feel it coming, just dropped like a hard ball on the hard wood of the dining room floor in the second-floor apartment she shares with her husband of 64 years. And, she broke it—her right arm, that is. The arm, that in those glory days of 1939–43 fired smokin' hot fastballs back to the plate at the famous Boston Garden where she was known as Schulzie, first "baseman" for the professional women's softball team, *The Boston Olympets*. Then, in the physical fitness of her youth, her right arm was rocket-propelled firm muscle fiber. Now, at 90-years-old it has worn the test of time, service, and gravity, with that once firm bulge now an inverted flap of skin hanging precariously beneath its bone. Her body is now war-torn from fighting all too many opponents: cancer, colostomy, colostomy reversal, hernia repair, and another nasty one called CHF or congestive heart failure from a leaking heart valve that continues to regurgitate her blood into her lungs. She is tired, bruised, old, and worn, and she is on the floor, limp, listless, and lifeless.

But, a strange thing happens there on the floor. She is suddenly, transformed back in time to that shining moment when she was a vital member of the *Boston Olympets*. She hears the roar of the crowd, feels the hard cement beneath her feet, long before *The Garden* floor would be famous for its parquet-tiled design, and she smells the stifling cigar-smoked laden air spewing from men like fire-breathing dragons dressed in their wide-brimmed hats. The sweat begins to pour from her as it dampens her red, white, and blue silk uniform. She is up at bat one more time. It is now her turn to turn the tide in the game. "Schulzie! Schulzie!" her teammates scream from the bench. Then she hears her now-deceased brother Al's voice shouting his pet name for her from the stands of heaven, "Go get 'em Wo-Wo!" (He always called her that because of her charmingly enthusiastic way of saying 'Whoaaaaaa!' whenever she got excited.) She hears his chant loud and clear: "Go. Go. Wo-Wo!" And, hearing his voice again, she jolts back to reality, and snaps back to consciousness.

It is at this moment that she realizes the pain has to be dealt with, and that there is yet another battle she will have to fight to win in overtime—the one to regain the use of her old playing arm to some semblance of normalcy for her age. She now knows that the time has come for *her* story to be told.

Team One:
The Schulzes

2

Glory-BE!
Marion Arrives

The sun shone down a little brighter on July 30th, 1917. Actually, it was a lot brighter, the hottest day of the year to be exact. In fact, according to her mother, Edie Mae, two horses died quickly in Malden Square that day of heat exhaustion. Though nearly nine decades would pass before the term global warming would ever be uttered, it was still a day that was far too hot for a woman to be in labor. But, Edie Mae was in labor—thank God—and the earth got to be a far better place that 30th of July. The first daughter and third child of seven from the union of Arthur and Edith Marion (a.k.a. Edie Mae) Schulze, arrived: Marion Edith Schulze was born.

Marion was a sweet-faced, beautiful baby girl with big brown eyes the size of softballs that glimmered with flecks of gold when she laughed—the kind of eyes that make a person instantaneously likeable to all who gaze upon her. Yet, this unassuming little girl would later prove to break new ground for womankind. She grew to be a toddler who did not enjoy doing the typical "girlie-girl" things of the 1920s, playing with dolls and dressing all frilly, pretty and pampered. No, that was and is not Marion. The original "tomboy," she much preferred playing ball with her two older brothers, Al and Frank, and her younger brother, Arthur (also known as Junie), and all the other boys in the neighborhood for that matter, near their modest three-bedroom cottage by the lumberyard and cow pasture on Eastern Avenue in Malden, Massachusetts.

"Ah, yes, those were the days," she so often says with a smile of fond remembrance breaking over her face, igniting a spark into those brown eyes, a switch that lights the window into her soul. "It wasn't like nowadays with kids on the computer or watching TV, I was always outside playing baseball, basketball, football, hide 'n' seek, or croquet with the boys, until my mother would come over by the cow pasture where I played to break up the game by yelling over: "'Marion, time to mind the babies.'"

Marion actually got teased about that all the time. In fact, the kids would just see her mother cross the street and they'd start the chant: "Marion, time to mind the babies." It seemed like that happened a lot, as her mother, Edith, was always a woman on the go-go-go, very active in her Protestant church, but, in typical Marion fashion, without attitude, she would immediately comply to her mother's wishes, drop her bat, and head for home to do her daughterly duty.

Though, being the oldest girl of seven children, it always seemed like there was a never-ending supply of babies to be minded. Marion was sandwiched between Al, Frank, and Junie. Then came her younger sister, Ruthie, and then much later, another sister and great friend in life, Avis, and yet another baby brother, Bobbie. It was these latter two siblings that Marion became a second mother to. Marion jokes, "After Ruthie was born, my mother told me, 'Marion, there won't be any more babies, I've had a hysterectomy.' Of course, I didn't even know what she meant by that word, I was only 16 and, back then, 16-year-olds didn't know anything about that sort of thing. But, anyway, I told my mother, "Ma, if there's any way you can have more babies, you'll find a way. And, sure enough she did! After her "hysterectomy" along came those two more babies, Avis and Bobbie."

All seven children, her parents, and grandmother on her mother's side, Sadie Linscott, lived in the modest three-bedroom home. Sadie's husband, Frank, a retired Buick car salesman had passed away quickly from a heart attack, so she came to live with her daughter's family. It was Marion, however, who took a shine to her, and she to Marion. They spent hours upon hours together talking, forming a bond that only a grandmother and granddaughter can know. It was Sadie, too, who taught her how to make mittens on four needles and turn knitting into an art form (a talent that family members would later benefit from with countless afghans and one-of-a-kind original, stunning baby sweaters and outfits). But, the person who really shaped her personality was her father who was the love of her early life. In those days, the husband was the sole provider, and her father and idol, Arthur, was the man of the house, an insurance salesman who toiled long hours into the nights writing policies and balancing clients and the books alike (something that Marion would later help out with when she became a teenager). It was her Dad she was most like, though. Whether it was gardening with him, tending to their tomatoes, or just learning how to fix things around the house, it was he whom she enjoyed being with the most. She definitely inherited his easygoing personality and that knack of puttering about because even up to the age of 89, she was the one who fixed anything broken in the house, from chairs to light fixtures, to programming their VCR. She was always way ahead of her time in that regard, never afraid of new technology, a woman's libber if you will, who could do any kind of "man's work," and actually do it better.

From her mother, Edie Mae, she inherited a life force and a love of gambling. (Not the kind of gambling that will get you in the slammer, of course, but just enough to bring a little joy and excitement to life.) For example, she loves to bet on the things that are near and dear to her heart, and does so even to this day—*sports!* What 90-year-old woman do you know can pick the winners on the college football cards and follows them like a religion? Marion does. She is actually quite good at it and has won on several occasions. Of course, she doesn't have a bookie or anything. It's just a little game she plays. And, boy does she like games! Always did. Marion loves to play any kind of board game, be it Monopoly, Sorry, Scrabble, Family Feud, Pass-the-Ace (a family favorite), and—of course—Bingo! She gets that from Edie Mae too.

One thing that she definitely did *not* get from her mother, though, is a love of dancing. But, then again, Marion's mother, Edie Mae, was the product of such. Her mother, Anastasia Hickey, was an actress and dancer in the early days of Boston. When she got pregnant and gave birth to Edie Mae, she was much too poor to care for a baby on an actress' salary, so she left her daughter on a woman's doorstep—that woman, was Sadie Linscott. Yes, Edie Mae was adopted. Though Sadie did have another child, a son by the name of Austin, he was much older than Edie. He had been away from his mother for years. Austin was a smart boy, who studied hard, got a good job, and moved to Virginia where he later got married. So, Sadie, at that point in life, turned all her attention to her new daughter who was left on her doorstep, Edie Mae. And Edie Mae, true to the circle of life, later in years took in Sadie on her doorstep, which is how Sadie ended up living with Edie Mae, her husband Arthur, and their seven children in that little white cottage on Eastern Avenue in Malden—the home where Marion grew up—the place she met her first coaches and teammates in life, her first ballpark to hone her baseball skills.

3

The 'Glory-ous'Fenway of Eastern Avenue

The old lumberyard on Eastern Avenue that was Marion's first training field didn't actually have Fenway Park's green monster, but it did have something else that might turn green and smell monstrous. In fact, hearing this story actually takes you back to a decade lost in time when girls and boys really did lead the simple life, way before Paris Hilton and Nicole Ritchie turned that phrase into a reality show. It was a time when cows might be in the road slowly going by you in a herd vs. the buzz of cars and SUVs whizzing by your head, the roar of horns replaced by the soft baritone of Moooooooooo.

If you listen hard enough, you can almost hear the clip-clop of their hooves striking the cobblestone streets.

Not far from Marion's home, there was a family by the name of the Shicks. They had a milk and bakery business. Naturally, that meant they had cows! Julius and Mary Shick were the two oldest siblings and they had to bring 12–15 cows past the Schulze home on Eastern Avenue.

As Marion says, "They would lead them in the middle of the street down past my home. Julius and Mary would take them all up Broadway to our little field a.k.a. The Malden City Lumber Company. Of course, there was wood and every-thing to build a home in that lumberyard, but there was also a little patch of green. My friends and I made a hole big enough in the fence so we could go over there when it was closed. When the Shicks' cows took over our field, though, that meant we were unable to play baseball until they were through grazing. After an hour or so, Mary would gather them all together and proceed to lead them home, which meant getting on Broadway, turning right at the intersection and past my house again. There was one big problem, as the cows always left what I would call "pancakes" behind them. So, when we played you had to be very careful not to step on one of those pancakes as you could slip and be in a real mess."

(Hmmmm, I wonder if the Red Sox would like to know this secret for sliding home!) If the Sox had known Marion then, however, they would have signed her. Just ask the other boys she played with. Marion—being the only girl who didn't throw like a girl—was always picked first for sides. This offers yet more evidence that just goes to prove that way back then even kids knew that having Marion on your team was a definite advantage to win the game—and you didn't need a coach to tell you that one.

If only Marion didn't need to go to school or mind the babies at home, she'd be at that wonderful patch of green till the cows came home. (No pun intended.) But, school—and babysitting—always seemed to get in the way of what she really wanted to do—PLAY BALL!

4

Some 'Glory-ous' Early Coaches

The blare of the loud horn was deafening as it echoed throughout the entire city of Malden. If it screeched twice—the sound of music to a kid—that was the equivalent of Barry Burbank, Dick Albert, and Pete Bouchard (all renowned Boston weathermen) screaming in your ear to roll over and go back to bed—the Malden school system's (circa 1920s) equivalent of a "no school" public service announcement.

In the Schulze household, however, that meant the bang of doors slamming in a royal scramble to get to the one and only bathroom for a family of 8 at that time. Then with a whoosh and a mad dash that makes *The Amazing Race* look like a snail's pace, all the kids would literally jump into layer-upon-layer of warm woolens and galoshes galore in the hopes of being first out the door for a day of sledding down the Hansen's hill off Eastern Ave.

When summer vacation came, however, off came the woolens, galoshes, and mittens. It was time for the annual Schulze family road trip. That's when the whole family would head north to visit Edie Mae's rich aunt, Avis, who lived in Dresden Mills, Maine.

"She had a lot of cows, chickens, and even a pig. I loved that trip, as we were able to see the farmhand milk the cows, feed the chickens, and even collect the eggs. It was a large farm and we had lots of land to play ball in."

But, soon the school bell would toll, and that's when you could find at least three of the then five Schulze kids walking to the Maplewood School, in stair-step height order.

"My two older brothers sort of looked after me. They were good brothers. Al, who was in the 5th grade, coached me along in baseball and basketball after school. Frank and I, well, we just didn't hit it off, as Frank was not one to really enjoy sports." Yet, she could always count on Frank and her special friend that she had in her brother, Al, to always be there for her whenever she needed them.

Marion's first day of school, however, pretty much set the tone for the rest of her life—***she did not cry***. She calmly watched her mother walk along home and just, well, adjusted.

"My first grade teacher was a woman by the name of Mrs. Genest. My third grade teacher was an 'old maid,' and I learned a lot more and she really did like me. Next came a woman named Mrs. Wilson. She was very strict and everyone tried to avoid her class, but, sure enough, I was in Mrs. Wilson's class … and the kids were right."

Of course, there were plenty of kids in the neighborhood to pass on this valuable information.

"One side of my street was two-family houses, and the other side had three single-family homes, one of them being ours. We would play games in the streets until the lights on the lampposts came on. Once, I remember when we had a lot of rain, our street flooded up like a small pond. All the kids were happy. We were able to go into the flooded street with no shoes and no stockings and have lots of fun."

Another flood of memories, of sorts, comes to Marion's mind: One of her earliest of friends, who also had to be in at night when the lights on the lampposts came on, was a little Italian girl by the name of Carmela. She was one of Marion's first friends. When she was about 8 or 9, they would walk to school together (when her brothers no longer needed to walk her). Marion enjoyed chatting it up with her along the way, however, there was one thing that Marion had a problem with, and that was when Carmela spoke.

"She was a very nice girl, but the only thing was, that, being Italian, she sort of had bad breath … the kind that really reeks of garlic."

With a slight smile and an ever so sweet little giggle, Marion confides, "I was glad in a way when she moved away early on. We only were friends for a short while because of that, but … that's probably why to this day, I don't like garlic."

Though Marion is not a gastronomic gourmet, one thing she learned very early on was how to cook for "just plain folks." In fact, that was one thing she would look forward to after a hard day at school. On the off days that her mother, Edie Mae, would not be home, she would look forward to cooking with the Julia Child of the Schulze household—Sadie.

5

The 'Glory-ous' Growing Years

The smell of Nana Linscott's Parker House dinner rolls was like no other. The aroma of bread in the oven infused the house with warmth and love. It was, however, a telltale sign that she and Marion had been in the kitchen baking, though not a speck of flour was anywhere to be found. "My mother would have been very upset if she came home with the church-ladies to the mess of flour on the table and countertops." That's why Sadie didn't come downstairs much to bake. Of course, it wasn't the only reason. That age-old disease, arthritis, was what kept her mostly confined to her upstairs bedroom. When she did sneak down to cook, though, it was an event resembling the Pillsbury Bake-Off! All the recipes were in her head and Marion gobbled them up in her memory banks just as quickly as Sadie Linscott's famous dinner rolls were gobbled up by the church-ladies—and you'd never know when they, or anyone else for that matter, would drop by.

You see, 1026 Eastern Avenue in Malden was a popular destination because of a popular woman—Edie Mae. It was Edie's love of music that brought the family together and many visitors to the house. Marion loved to listen to her mother play piano. Marion's love of music consisted mostly of her Sunday school hymns, but to her mother, Edie Mae, music was what coursed through her veins. Whether it was dancing to a polka (her favorite), gliding on the dance floor to a beautiful waltz, or having her kids line up with their instruments to play for her friends, it was what she thrived on.

As Marion reminisced, "I remember my brother Al was the drummer, and Frank the clarinetist, and soon I became the family's trombone player. In order to entertain the ladies from church, one by one, we would play our instruments. I loved music a lot, but I did not ever enjoy her love of dancing, maybe because I was a tomboy and loved sports so much better."

So much so did Marion love sports that she was always out the door whenever she could to play ball with the boys. There wasn't much time for her to play that, however, as she was the prime babysitter for the entire family. History seemed to repeat itself of sorts, as that is what it was like for her father, Arthur, too, as a child. You see, when he was young, he also did not have much time to play. His father had owned a drugstore in Revere and Arthur always had to hurry home from school to help in any way he could. He was not able to play many sports as he had a paper route and many, many chores that kept him busy. It seems, that Marion and her father, had more than just chores in common, though.

"I loved my father very much, as he taught me how to work with so many tools. I remember, when I first learned how to drive, he made sure I could change a flat tire. (Something rare in those days … a woman behind the wheel, let alone changing a tire!) Anyway, he wouldn't let me get behind the wheel until I could prove that I could get the wheel off—lug nuts and all—and put it back on again. He also taught me how to repair many things that needed to be fixed, and how to work in the vegetable garden and trim the hedges that lined our house."

That was much better than the job her brothers got … cleaning the chicken coop. She'd take gardening and yard work to that job any day.

It was when toiling in the garden, that her Dad and Marion had many meaningful talks. Like any good father, he always made sure to tell her that she was a very good girl and that he was very grateful that she developed a lot of good habits around both children and adults. They had a special bond those two. Her Dad was such a hard worker for the family, and throughout his years had several different jobs, most of the time holding two down at once. (Something that Marion did later on in life, as well.) One such position was when he was the manager of the Fisk Rubber Company in Boston. That job gave both Marion and her siblings much joy.

"Lots of times he would be the only one working on a Sunday in the plant, and he would take my brothers and me with him. They had a big slide where the tires would be placed to go down the chute to the salesroom below. Well, we would go up to the top of the stairs and slide down while he was doing a little work. We sure loved that and looked forward to it."

Unfortunately, that job closed and he was out of work. Soon, he became a salesman for *Sears*. But, it was his last job that really solidified their special relationship, when he became a salesman for the *Metropolitan Life Insurance Company*. As it happened, this new career provided much inspiration for some very important life lessons that Marion would later encounter, but first she had to *insure* her own place in time, and learn a few of those lessons on her own—courtesy of the Malden school system and the school of hard knocks.

6

Some 'Glory-ous' Growing Pains

Marion was growing up, but the trouble was, her body was too. She not only was growing and changing physically and mentally, but her responsibilities were growing by leaps and bounds as well. She would daydream at her desk in junior high of playing ball on that little patch of heavenly green in the lumberyard. Then, suddenly, without warning, she would be startled out of this stuporous state by the sound of Edie Mae's voice—"Marion, time to mind the babies." Then, she would have to get back to reality and the many tasks at hand—schoolwork and '*home*'work.

She wore many different hats for an 11-year-old. (And, I don't mean the Easter hats that she was forced to wear to look good for the Protestant church-ladies who would come to visit her house.) And, as in most families, things weren't always Easter-Sunday-picture-perfect in the Schulze household either.

"My parents had a great relationship, but like a lot of families, they had a lot of arguments. My father, being the only breadwinner, gave my mother the money to buy groceries, clothing and so forth. But, once he got really upset with her because she claimed she always needed more money to buy more groceries. After a while, she changed her story to say she needed the money to buy a girdle. Well, it seemed to my father that she was buying an awful lot of girdles, and that made him really upset."

But, not as upset as Marion. She didn't like to hear her parents argue, and, at the age of 11, she was the daughter, sister, and babysitter/part-time mother to all the younger children. She felt she had to protect them, but that didn't always work.

"Once when I was minding little Junie, he got away from me in the yard very quickly and was run over by a car. Thank goodness he had no broken bones, only some bruises and scrapes. My mother was very, very upset with me."

Now, even though Edie Mae put Marion in charge of the other children a lot of the time, she still was a very loving mother herself, a good woman, and they enjoyed many a shopping expedition together as well as searching out bargains. It was only that Edie Mae just liked to be out and about. (Maybe that was because she married so young at the tender age of 16.) She taught Marion more than just bargain hunting though. She taught her some important lessons as well: to consider other people, be helpful, and to always be selective of friends—all good advice.

But, as she headed into puberty, it wasn't Edie Mae who gave her the advice she needed. It was, once again, her confidante, Sadie—her warm and fuzzy, wonderful grandmother.

"She knew when I was going to go into the menstrual period of life, and she explained it all to me."

What Marion didn't know was when this menstrual period of life would hit her—during band practice.

"I was a member of the band and I was the only girl who played the trombone. The other two were boys. (This is yet another instance of a woman ahead of her time. How many young girls would choose to play the trombone in the early 1930s?) Anyway, I remember getting up from practice and my girlfriend, Violet, telling me there was something on the back of my skirt. We went to the bathroom and she told me it must be what my grandmother had told me about." Marion gives a little chuckle, "We covered the spots up with markers."

Speaking of spots, there was another time in junior high when it came time for the band to play in a competition. Marion actually got to be pretty good at the trombone, as Edie Mae had arranged for her to have lessons with a local music teacher, named Mr. Gillespie. Marion was so good that she actually played both in the band and the orchestra.

"We were going to competition to see which band would get a trophy. Our music teacher made sure we looked our very best. Our uniforms were all cleaned and spotless, so we would look our best when we tried out for the contest. My good friend, Lois, who played clarinet in the band, was sitting alongside me on the bus. Well, there we were riding in the bus on our way to the contest when Lois got sick, and, without any warning, vomited all over her uniform and partly on mine. I thought my bandleader was going to have a heart attack because she was so mad at poor Lois. We had many laughs over this, as we talked about it for weeks after that."

But, as it happens in life, that laughter quickly turned to tears. What started out as a bright day in the life of a student in junior high quickly transformed into a nightmare as the sun set. Marion's beloved grandmother, Sadie, took a turn for the worse one evening, and, she passed away into the night without the fanfare Sadie so deserved.

Marion, to this day, speaks of her in the most loving of terms, and with a frown on her face and the faintness of moisture in her eyes, she describes her pain.

"I watched the medical people come and put her in a body bag and take her away. It really hurt because I came to love her so much, and she loved me dearly as well. I never did tell my parents that I witnessed that. They knew how close we both were. I was sad for quite a while after she passed away."

Marion's confidanté was now gone. She would simply have to figure out the answers to life's mysteries and quandaries on her own, and, they would soon come—very fast, indeed. High school was on the horizon.

7

The 'Glory-ous' Fast Times at Malden High???

The year was 1932, about five decades shy of the release in theaters of the movie: *Fast Times at Ridgemont High, a* film about teens in a California high school living life in the fast lane of the 1980s (and I don't mean the highway) with drugs, booze, and sex. So, the question is: "Did we, as a moral society, progress in that quantum leap of time?"

If you listen to what being a young, pretty, brown-eyed brunette at Malden High School in Malden, Massachusetts was like for Marion Schulze back in the early '30s … well, I'll just let you judge for yourself. The answer is a resounding one.

The country was still in the throes of the Great Depression, but, somehow, miraculously, most people weren't. Families pulled together. Kids wore second-hand clothes with no complaints. Shoes weren't something to collect and throw away when out of fashion. If you had a hole in your one-and-only pair, the local cobbler down the street fixed it for pennies. Families ate dinner 'round the table with lively discussions, only to retire to the "parlor" to play Monopoly or other popular board games, as was the case with the Schulzes of Eastern Avenue. Money was tight. Music was light … ballads mostly, and Bing Crosby was a huge favorite. Sometimes, *The Jack Benny* show or *Amos 'n' Andy* could be heard on the big box—the radio—that is, as television was not in most of America's living rooms yet. The President was Herbert Hoover. And, if you were rich enough to see a movie, Wallace Beery and Jackie Cooper's names could be seen on the brightly-lit marquee of Main Street, America, starring in: *The Champ.*

1932 was also the year that Marion Schulze entered Malden High School, and by graduation day in 1936, a "champ" is exactly what she would prove to be. But, like any true champion, the way to a winning attitude and title involves a lot of practice and hard work with a healthy dose of a few character-building lessons thrown in along the way.

As is the case with most teen-agers, even ones back then, peer pressure was a fact of life. Marion, however, was always a woman who knew who she was and what she did and did not like. Of course, back then, high school wasn't like it was portrayed in *Fast Times at Ridgemont* High with drugs, booze, and sex. Back then, that kind of behavior was not even heard of, never mind tolerated. No, the pace of life was *a lot slower*. The only vice a teen was tempted by his or her peers to try was smoking. That was the evil of the day in the '30s.

"I know a lot of my friends did smoke, though, and they wanted me to try it, but I did not, as I did not like the smell of smoke."

Again, Marion proved she was ahead of her time: a woman who knew who she was. She always knew what was and what was *not* for her. She always played by the rules, not only in sports, but also in the classroom. She was a good student in high school, and when she wasn't on the basketball court, she could be found in the library. The only trouble she ever got into in high school had to do with the dress code. Boys had to wear shirts and ties all the time. As for the girls, well, they were ladies, ladies who never swore a cuss word and whose prim and proper school attire consisted strictly of skirts and blouses or regular dresses. (You have to remember now, that it was the Depression era, and times were tough ... money was tight.) Marion always had good, clean clothes, however, even if they were hand-me-downs from the older daughters of Edie Mae's church ladies. What she didn't have a lot of at the time was nylons to wear with those dresses. (These were not pantyhose, either, as they were not invented yet.) The following is the extent of where Marion's rebellious, teen-aged, high school persona came into play.

"No slacks, whatsoever, were allowed, as that was a no-no. We always had to wear nylon stockings, which I hated. So, one day, I went to school without any. Sure enough, I was caught and sent to the principal's office where I was told to go home, get my stockings, and return to class."

And, that she did. Marion always went to class ... well ... almost always. Only if it was history (which she didn't like) did she skip a class once-in-a-while.

"My hiding place was in the girl's locker room where I hid in one of the stalls. I never did get caught."

As it turned out, the locker room is where Marion spent a lot of time in high school. However, she didn't think it would be at first. When high school first started, she thought she would be spending most of her time with the school band. That dream quickly vanished. She had honed her horn-playing skills quite nicely, thanks to the music teacher Edie Mae had found her. But, a notice went out that girls could not play in the high school band—only boys were allowed. That meant the end to Marion's musical career. Her father sold her trusty Vega trombone to buy a coat, as there were seven children in the family to feed and clothe, and that shiny brass fetched quite a pretty penny and a darn good coat.

But, that was okay. Marion recovered, quite nicely in fact. The loss of being told that girls could not play in the band only made her more determined to excel in another area she loved—sports.

Marion quickly turned her attention to basketball. At this time in history, high schools did not have any girls' baseball or softball teams, as she would have been very happy then. But, Marion set her sights on conquering the basketball court, thanks to a favorite teacher, and it was there that she became a legend.

"I had a gym teacher by the name of Mrs. Johnson. She gave me such a liking for basketball, and she taught me well. Also, one of my best friends was a little Italian girl by the name of Teddy Rinaldi. Her real name was Theodora. She was one grade ahead of me in school. She gave me some very good advice and pointers on how to play. She told me to try hard and soon I would be captain the following year."

This premonition soon became a reality with Marion's hard work, lots of after-school practices, and some pretty fast-and-fancy footwork on the court. By her senior year in high school, Marion had, indeed, become the Captain. The Malden High basketball team soon won the league championship and received a beautiful trophy.

She combined her love of basketball with academics, even in the summers between high school years.

"Oh my glory!" gleams a reminiscing Marion. "I almost forgot. In Malden, we had a contest, a writing contest, to form our own basketball teams to enter a league. I organized a team in which I coached and played. We were given the right to use the school gym. I got a team together and I named the team: *The Co-Eds*. We won the city title and I won the highest trophy for having the highest score in the city."

When not on the court in the summers, Marion could be found playing girls volleyball in the city's parks, and, in typical fashion, breaking new ground (again, ahead of her time) for girls playing baseball on the boys' teams. Marion was not just a pretty face with great legs. She showed them that she could play their games too—and beat them at 'em, to boot!

"Each park had a girl's volleyball team and we would be able to play against other parks to find out who would be the winner. At the time, there was also not any girls' softball team, and, being that baseball was my favorite sport, they allowed me to play on the boys' team in the park. I was the only girl. We would travel from park to park to find out what park had the best baseball team."

Marion excelled at whatever sport she entered, that was certain. But, not only, did she succeed at sports, she also was a winning daughter in high school and on the home front, as well.

"My father taught me how to proof his insurance debit plans for the whole week, balanced right to the penny, as we had to find out where my or his mistakes were. Once a week, on Thursdays, I helped him balance the books. That was in my Junior Year. My father allowed me to have a raise, and that was $5.00 a week. I was very happy with that."

Marion's father, and brothers, Al and Arthur, a.k.a Junie, were always there for her too. They attended all her athletic games, and she, likewise, was always there for them, but, in particular, she was there for her special guy, her Dad. Consider this introduction into a teen-ager's driver's education:

"My father broke his ankle on the job once, and I had to drive him around on his insurance routes. In those days, people would pay him a small portion of their insurance policies, and that meant a lot of stop-and-go driving. That is how I learned to drive. It was hard for him, but with my help, he collected all the money from his customers."

Of course, amidst all these hectic high-school happenings, Marion balanced minding her younger siblings between games and practices. (Also, a new baby to mind was added to the Schulze family. A baby girl, Avis, was born while Marion was in high school.) Babysitting might have taken its toll on Marion's social life, but Marion never complained.

"The library was where I went to read a good novel or to study a subject I liked, like geography. And, when I wasn't playing sports, I was with my friends Gracie Fowler or Teddy Rinaldi."

Then came senior year, and the traditional rite of passage that most teen-aged girls look forward to, the one that encompasses all the excitement, girlish wonderment, and awe that can be summed up into one word ... *prom.*

Even then, Marion, as usual, was a girl unlike others ... a girl who knew herself.

"I did not go to any dances, not even to my prom. I was asked, but I made an excuse, as I did not know how to dance, and did not even think about getting a gown for the occasion. I suppose a lot of them thought I was odd, as a lot of them made plans to attend."

Prom came and went and that was okay with Marion. It was the future she looked forward to. Marion graduated from Malden High School in 1936.

"It was four wonderful years, and I made a lot of friends and was very popular. It was sad, however."

Marion had hoped to attend college to become a physical education teacher. But, being the Depression era, and being the oldest girl in the Schulze household of seven siblings, college was a no-go. Forever the optimist, however, Marion made the best of it—and turned to what she loved: baseball. (To illustrate this, is an excerpt that her brother wrote about Marion during this time in her life):

> "There was a man by the name of Bill Dempsey, Sr., who was director of Physical Education in the city of Malden. He was also in charge of the Semi-Pro Baseball Team called the Malden Twi. Former college baseball stars and the best players from all over played on this team. Mr. Dempsey knew talent and had the foresight to know that some girls could play sports as well as any boy. He took my sister, Marion Schulze, on his team to play first base. Everywhere they played (locally and places like Gloucester and many New Hampshire towns) there were large crowds eager to see a girl player competing with the boys."

It was clear to Marion that change was foreshadowed beyond the horizon of high school and the ballparks she played. "I was unable to go to college, so a lot of my friends sort of disappeared and were on their own, or married."

That was just fine. The future had a plan for Marion—all in due time. Good things would come slowly for her, especially in matters of the heart, as fast times, (other than fast balls thrown at her to catch), well, that's just not Marion's style. The future, however, would involve the two things she loved most in the world—sports and family—and they came in that order ... well, almost. Actually, it was more a marriage of both, literally, that is, as you shall see.

Team Two:
The Olympets

8

The Glory of Fate and Plates

The torch was passed: in Malden and far, far away.

The students graduating from MHS that year were poised to go out into the world. Simultaneously, in a world far away from this little suburb of Boston, the ***1936 Summer Olympics*** began. The ***Games of the XI Olympiad*** officially heralded the introduction of the Olympic Torch bringing the Olympic Flame by relay from Olympia to Berlin, Germany. It was, truly, history in the making. Adolf Hitler, the German Chancellor, viewed the competitions as his golden opportunity to promote the Nazi party's ideology of Aryan superiority, but, the Greek Gods of Olympus shone down, and, as fate would have it, an American upset dominated the games. Jesse Owens, an African-American, won four gold medals that year. It was also these Olympic games that debuted the sport of basketball in competition. In a twist of irony and fate, that same year, in Malden, Massachusetts, a young fraulein, "Schulzie," would cause an upset with an established basketball coach.

Marion, the lean, strong-legged, pretty brunette with big-brown softball-saucered-eyes, was now a new MHS graduate. She was eager to play ball and get a job, (not necessarily in that order) but there was no prospect in sight on both horizons. It was summer, though, and the temperature was soaring. Babysitting kept her busy. Now that she graduated, she revived her role as part-time (and more) mother to her two new younger siblings: two-year-old, Avis, and new baby brother, Bobbie. The 3 R's of reading, 'riting, and 'rithmetic, took a back seat to the 3 C's of cleaning, changing diapers, and cooking. The cooking, she enjoyed, though, as being in the kitchen brought back memories of Sadie:

"Three or four times during the summer, my Dad and two older brothers (Al and Frank) would go clam digging down to Revere Beach. They would come home with a couple of large buckets of clams. My mother and I would steam them up in a big, boiling pot of water while we cooked up some corn on the cob on the side. Then we would all eat to our heart's content."

But, content she was not with the fact that she did not have a "real" job that paid. Soon, summer turned to fall, and a local woman, who ran a Day-Care Center on Sheafe Street for preschoolers, needed a driver to pick-up the children in the mornings. Marion went to see the woman and she hired her on the spot. The only trouble was that the job only lasted six months as the day-care had closed. That left Marion without a paycheck yet again. But, not to worry … fate, plates (china ones, to be specific), and a phone call would soon change her world.

She received a telephone call one day from a nice, young man by the name of James "Jimmie" Rush. (He, likewise, served as the captain of Everett High School's baseball and basketball teams. After he graduated, he played shortstop and second base for a semi-pro baseball team called the Everett Cardinals. Everett was the next town over from Malden.) Jimmie Rush, a local star in his own right, was now at a crossroads looking for a new challenge in his life. His baseball career had ended, and he now was given the opportunity to coach and manage a girl's basketball team in Everett called: The *Collins Club*. He had heard through the grapevine (and local newspapers) about what a good player Marion Schulze was, and he knew she, too, had been the captain of her high school's basketball team just a few years prior. He, matter-of-factly, over the telephone offered her a position to play on his newly formed team. Well, she was thrilled to say the least, and she started as soon as she could.

In her usual fashion, she gave it all she had, scoring points, etc., but she still felt that no matter how many baskets she made or how hard she tried, he always had something to say about the way she played. She felt she just could *not* make this new coach happy. She was puzzled about the way he acted, and would even lament to the other girls in the locker-room. "I can't figure it out," she said. "I just cannot seem to make this coach happy, no matter what I do." On the sidelines, he would continue to instruct her. But, whenever he did, her face would flush (and it wasn't from running on the court). Marion had a big c-r-u-s-h on the c-o-a-c-h—and the courtship was about to begin.

Now, around this same time she had landed a new job in a china shop that made plates. She was hired as a plate-painter who painted the patterns on these delicate dishes. As it happens, the china factory was located on a busy street corner that served as a bus stop as well. Marion could be found waiting at this corner bus stop to see Jimmie Rush's bus go by on his way to work. A wave here or there would ensue.

After several dozen-or-so bus-stop-waves, games, practices, and drives to pick Marion up to and from practices to games, and games to practices, they became an item—and remained an item for many years. (Five years to be exact, a game truly in overtime!)

Over-time, though, is exactly how Marion's sports career and the relationship blossomed. Jimmie Rush, the thin, good-looking, steely-blue-eyed gentleman/ coach of Scottish-English descent became a big part of her life. He was a man no one could not like, quiet and unassuming, gentle and kind-hearted. The Schulze family embraced him right away. As for what the Rush side thought of Marion, well, Jimmie's father, James Honeywell Rush, liked her all right. However, he was pretty much like his son, as he, too, was a quiet man. He was a hard worker who worked for the Dupont Paint Company in Boston in the laboratory. It was Jimmie's mother, Veronica, who was another story. Marion was a Protestant and the Rushes, being strict Catholics didn't think kindly of her. Veronica loved the church and its priests. She was the kind of woman who donated money and food willingly and generously to her local parish and missionaries abroad, therefore, she was not very fond of the fact that her one-and-only son was dating a Protestant girl, one named Schulze, at that! But, still, they dated, and dated, and dated, no matter what Veronica had to say or how she acted. Jimmie, quite literally, stood behind his new sweetheart, whether she was up at bat at home plate or just plain at home going to bat for her in her defense with his mother. Even though Marion's sports star would appear to shine more brightly than his in 1939 and 1940, and even though Jimmie's soul (in his mother's eyes) was at risk, Marion was, and is, to this very day, his soulmate, whose personality meshes and fits with his like a glove—well, actually it's more like a mitt.

9

In the League
The Glory Years: The Olympets

July 4th, 1939 was officially named as Lou Gehrig day at Yankee Stadium. His uniform, #4, was retired that day. The baseball legend, the greatest player of the twentieth century, would also forever be known as the greatest first baseman of all time. He was nicknamed: **The Iron Horse** for his durability. On this day in history, he gave his now famous "Luckiest Man in the World" speech.

Also in 1939, the red-white-and-blue-flag-waving-Oh-My-Glory-spouting, Marion Schulze, also wore a red-white-and-blue uniform—#4—and also played first baseman (or basewoman) for the #1 women's professional softball team: *The Boston Olympets*. In its heyday, this women's spitfire of a league played against—and won—Babe Ruth's NY team in Madison Square Garden. (Guess this just added yet another chapter to the Boston/NY rivalry!)

Marion, as one of *The Olympets*, always gave every game her all. She was then (and is now) the female version of **The Iron Horse.** The years between 1939 and 1943 were, for Marion, a very special time in her life … a moment of glory, a flash of fame, like Lou Gehrig, to be the "Luckiest 'Wo-Wo'-man in the World." Marion, like her male counterpart, was known then (and now) for her durability: a woman who never gives up and never lets her teammates down.

As the saying goes, however, this is the story of how it all went down. It is the tale of how there was a women's professional softball *league of their own* before there was: *A League of Their Own:* the movie … before names like Geena Davis, Madonna, Rosie O'Donnell, and Tom Hanks made the all-women's team, *The Racine Belles,* a household name. But, it was little known names, who were local stars. These are the women who have never had celebrities portray their lives—but they could have—if fate had not thrown them a curve ball in the crossroads of their young lives. They are the unsung names of *that* league: Dottie Green, Millie Mooney, Mary Pratt, Clara Chiano, Rosemary Boyle, and many,

many more, along with their coach, Jack Harris, and—of course—Marion (Wo-Wo Schulzie) Schulze. These are the women whose names and stories deserve to be told—and one of them will—in her own words:

"Walter Brown, who owned the Boston Garden at that time, wanted something to run in the summer months when the Garden was usually empty. With that in mind, he asked Howie McHugh, who did all the publicity for the Garden, to form a professional Girl's Softball Team that had already been organized in other states. So, Howie ran an ad in *The Boston Herald* that said any girl who wanted to try out for the team needed to report to the Garden on a certain date. At Jimmie's urging, he told me to go and try out. He said that I was good enough to compete, and he drove me to the Garden in his old, black '38, Dodge sedan. Off we went. Well, when I arrived, I could not believe my eyes ... so many girls of all ages had also shown up. There must have been between 200 and 300 girls ready to try out. That meant Howie needed help. So, he got a hold of a friend by the name of Jack Harris, a former Olympic hockey player who just happened to live in the same town as Howie, and he (Jack) later became our coach, while Howie then became our general manager. The girls were later separated into teams by ability: *The Totem Poles*, *The Gardenias*, and *The Olympets* (or *Pets* as we were known.) *The Totem Poles* and *Gardenias* were to be known as the Minor League teams who would feed into the Boston Garden when needed. Now, I was told that I made the top team, and I was thrilled to play in the Garden before a lot of fans. You have to remember that back then the Garden floor was hard cement, and that meant that sliding into the plate was a very rare thing at indoor softball games. I was paid $5 a game. Of course, though, we didn't know how much each one of us made, as they didn't tell us that. Add to that the fact that, being girls, we played in our little red shorts, so almost every girl on the team sported black and blue marks on her leg ... and we didn't have any protective equipment either! Besides our shorts, our uniform had had red, white, and blue lettering across the front of the white background shirt that spelled out *Olympets*. Each one had their number on the back. I was #4. We played in leather-laced sneakers ... there were no Nikes back then. We had beautiful yellow satin jackets when we played our away games. Anyway, Jack Harris worked with me a lot, as he was training me to play first base, and that was all new to me. They had bought me a beautiful, new, first base mitt, a special mitt with no fingers. Our team consisted mostly of girls who were college students and the other group worked for a living. That's what I was ... a working girl. Soon, the Olympets were ready to play against teams all over New England. One of our team members was a girl by the name of Dottie Green. And, believe me, she could have been a twin to the girl who played the character of Dottie Hinson in *A League of Their Own*, played by Geena Davis. The girl that played our third base was Rosemary Boyle, a college student from Framingham, MA. The shortstop was a girl named Millie Mooney, and boy could she throw a ball! Whoooooaaaaaa! *She was better than any boy that I ever saw!* She had an arm like a bullet, and I hated to see the ball coming, as I was the one who had to catch it at first! She threw so hard that I used to get bone bruises from Millie's fastball! Next, we had a little Italian girl named Clara Chiano, but we named her Gabby, as she gabbed and gabbed all the time. I became the first baseman, and I was not that bad of a hitter, and I always did my best. The League did very well, as good ol' Howie did a lot of publicity for us. We played teams from all over, even Canada, but one trip that Howie organized for us was to have our team go to New York and play in Madison Square Garden against one of New York's best teams. We got there by train and were to return by boat. We were put up in a hotel with three to four girls to a room. One of the games we played, we lost, and another we won. The one we lost was because the New York team had hired a real professional pitcher to pitch the whole nine innings and she was untouchable. Anyway, the next day we were invited to go to the World's Fair with *all expenses paid!* That was a time I will never forget. When we went to leave New York, the boat was much bigger than what I would call a boat. While leaving the harbor, from a short distance, one of the girl's hollered out, Hey, there's the Statue of Liberty! I had never seen it before, so I ran over to the window and watched and watched *The Statue* until I could not see it any more. 'Oh, my Glory!' I said, as my eyes welled-up."

Little did Marion know how memorable these years (1938–1940) would become for her. She was unaware that the movie *A League of Their Own* would parallel her team, *The Olympets*, and would actually end up having some of the players from her team go on to *The Racine Belles* of that movie fame—she being one of those women who could have been portrayed in it as well.

The New York-Boston game was also of particular significance, as the closer the game got when it came to the score, the more the crowd cheered. It was her turn. She was up at bat, stance ready, with her grip clutched steadfastly down on her bat. There she was with her bruised knees in her little-red-satin shorts. Suddenly, she heard a loud familiar voice chanting from behind the plate: "Go. Go.

Wo-Wo … Go. Go. Wo-Wo." She didn't need to turn to see who it was. She knew just by that name alone that it was her beloved big brother, Al, who had come to see her all the way from Boston to New York. Just as she was about to swing, another one of "*The* Pets" yelled to her, "Hey, Schulzie, isn't that your boyfriend?" Yes, Al and Jimmie had both come to see their special girl play ball in the big city. She was struck wondering how in the world did they get there (all while getting a base hit to help win the game.) Well, at the time, Al had worked for a bakery and had the use of the company "Cushman" truck. So, he and Marion's other special guy, Jimmie Rush, had driven all day to come and see their girl play in the Big Apple.

Later that evening, "the boys" wanted to take her out on the town to see the bright neon lights of Broadway, as Al had always wanted to see the famous *Cab Calloway Cotton Club Revue*. (This was a club that had opened first in the heart of Harlem owned by a prominent bootlegger and gangster. Later, it was relocated to Broadway and 48th street. Its nightlife was known for its "racist imagery of the times," and featured the jumpin'jive sounds of big-band jazz greats like Dizzie Gillespie, Duke Ellington, Louis Armstrong, and the Hi-De-Ho tootin,' Minnie-the-Moocher famed crooner himself, Cab Calloway. The dancers and strippers strutted their stuff around tables of whites-only patrons. This was surely a place that the "Modest Maid Marion" would, most certainly, feel, definitively, out of place.) Al and Jimmie wanted to go, but it wouldn't be that easy. Marion needed permission from her manager, Howie McHugh, in order to go out for the evening (even though she was with her brother and boyfriend.) Howie treated his *Pets* like a doting father. It happened that the other girls in the hotel were having quite a time, throwing things around and such in a pajama party, and Marion, well, she was just glad to get out of there. But, Howie had said she could go—if and only if—she brought one of the other girls along with her. So, she chose Rosemary Boyle to "double date" with her for the evening. She had never in her wildest dreams imagined what would await them at *The Cotton Club*. Marion, being the shy, green, girl who had never been in such a smoky, seedy place was like a fish out of water, a country bumpkin out in the jungle of the big city. (She laughs that special giggle of hers when she recalls the story and her aged-brown eyes begin to form that characteristic upward tilt with the little twinkle in them that tells you that something good is about to be told):

"It was sort of a what-cha-call-it—**sexy** place." (She cringes her shoulders upward as her eyes shut with embarrassment as she says *the* word.) The girls danced in skimpy outfits … sort of what you would see on that show today: *Dancing with the Stars*. The four of us didn't even drink. We only had *Coca-*

Colas. Anyway, this girl comes over and dances by our table and ... whooooaaa, all of a sudden she drops to the ground by the side of the table, like they do on that show. (The modest, maid Marion was shocked, stunned, and in awe to say the least.) Well, I felt this thing touch my shoulder and wondered what it was. When I turned around, it was my brother Al, reaching over me trying to get a better glimpse of the girl in the skimpy outfit lying there on the floor. Then, like I said, we weren't even drinking. We had been there for only about an hour when our waiter came over to us to give us our tab. It came to $13. Well, either Al or Jimmie only had $100 bill on them. I can't remember which one it was. So, we gave the waiter the $100. (The waiters there were all blacks at the time, as the Club did not allow blacks in as patrons.) Well, the waiter took the $100 and never came back with our change. My brother Al went to the manager and they asked him to point out the waiter. Al happened to remember who he was. The manager asked his employee why he never gave his party of four back their change. The waiter, in reply, said that he thought the balance was his tip. (In those days of pre-WW II, that would have been a small fortune!) Well, with that, we finally got our change back and back to the hotel Rosemary and I went while Jimmie and Al boarded the ol' *Cushman Truck* for the long drive back to Boston that same night."

The whole New York experience was quite a memory for Marion, but in her mind, all the glitz, glory, and fame that the Big Apple provided could not compare to what was about to come her way.

The 1940 Boston Olympets. Marion Schulze, a.k.a. "Schulzie" (or "Wo-
Wo" to her brother, Al) is in the back row, third from the left.

Marion in her glory years.

FEMALE FOXX—Marion Schulze, Malden girl, is the flossiest fielder in women's softball ranks. She'll play for Olympets tonight against Spaulding girls at Garden.

Boston Evening American Photo

In this clipping from the Boston Evening American, Marion is compared to Jimmie Foxx, the Hall of Fame first baseman for the Boston Red Sox in the 1930s and early 1940s. (Photo courtesy of *Boston Herald*.) The clipping below is from Marion's scrapbook, source unknown.

7—Sorry, Mildred, but SPEED-RAY says "you're out." Mildred Mooney, Pets shortstop, just misses beating out a hit by a step. Marian Schultz, first baseman, has the ball nicely covered and if Mildred is opening her mouth to protest it's going to do her no good—the SPEED-RAY never misses.

"The Newlyweds"
Mr. & Mrs. James F. Rush on their wedding day:
September 5, 1943.

The Rush children (left to right): Edmund, Patricia, and James, Jr.

Marion's beloved father and mother: Arthur and Edith Schulze

Marion sitting with her in-laws: Veronica and James Rush

10

The 'Glory-ous' Dating Game Years

History pressed on in 1941 with the slap of the Nazi's Gestapo boots vividly heard marching into country after European country. It was also the year that the United States was drawn into the world's political turmoil. On December 7th, 1941, then U.S. President, Franklin Delano Roosevelt, declared it a day that would live in infamy. In a surprise attack on our fleet anchored at Pearl Harbor, Hawaii, the Japanese (who had aligned themselves with the Germans) launched 181 torpedo and dive-bombers that decimated our American naval base and its military installations. There was no ambivalence about it—the United States was now thrust full throttle into World War II. Soon, it would be *our* boys who would be off to fight in a foreign land; it would be our men whose blood would be shed to stop the spread of Nazism.

Meanwhile, the romance between Jimmie & Marion was also on the march, but at a much slower pace than the political world. Slow and steady, that was Jimmie Rush's strategy to win the girl. It had now been about three years since they met, three years of going to ballgames together, three years of going to Joe & Nemo's for hot dogs after those games, three years of long walks on Revere Beach (punctuated literally by punches, albeit harmless, flirty punches in the arms), and three years of building a solid friendship like no other. Marion knew he was the guy she wanted to marry.

"He was a great coach. He had good manners and no bad habits. He did not drink and he did not smoke."

The feeling was mutual on his part. He was crazy about this girl. He just had a hard time showing it, as he was, as Marion puts it: "a shy, quiet fellow."

One night, as he they were walking back to the car after an Olympets game at the Garden, he noticed there was a note stuck under the windshield of his old, black Dodge. It was addressed to "Schulzie" and placed there by one of her many fans that followed the team from city to city, even all the way to Montreal, Canada. That was the moment that Jimmie knew he had competition and that it was time for him to pick up the pace. But, that would prove to be a hard thing to do. Becoming more than friends was difficult when Jimmie's mother didn't want them to be any more than that. After all, he was her only child, her only son. Veronica had lost another son, as Jimmie's twin had died at the age of three in an unfortunate incident where he had accidentally choked on a bean. This incredible gut-wrenching loss made Veronica that much more protective of Jimmie, and this hurdle made it impossible for him to find another woman who could win over his mother's heart and acceptance.

Jimmie, in his usual fashion, tread softly in these waters, never making waves, but keeping both women on an even keel at the same time. When it came to his mother, he tried to make a statement about his affection for Marion in an understated manner, carefully trying to gently nudge her into the Rush family outings. And, being an understanding woman, Marion would go along for the ride, literally taking a backseat to Veronica.

"We often took his mother, father, and aunt Mae (who also lived with them) to visit relatives. Jimmie always made sure that I was included in all the family affairs. I remember on one occasion the car was full of relatives, but he told his mother that I **had** to go and be included, so he went and got a small footstool, and I sat on that, right behind him all the way to Portsmouth, NH." (Now, that's the literal translation of a good woman behind every man. You also have to remember that these were the days before there were seatbelt laws and limits on the amount of people you could physically fit in a car. It was a time when driving to Portsmouth, NH from Malden, MA was the equivalent of Columbus setting off to find the New World. It took hours!)

And that was what awaited Marion, a New World soon to come her way in 1943. But, she wasn't consumed with the thought of a promise of a future with Jimmie. She, as she is now, was a patient person, and she knew that all good things take time. She had been working at a job in the United States Engineers Office in Boston (which just happened to be located near Fenway Park.) She had been there a couple of years now, ever since the china shop had closed. It paid very well. She started out by copying blueprints of buildings that were being built by the government. Soon she was promoted to a very unique position.

"My boss was a pilot and his job was to photograph many sections along the coast. With the war on, this was needed in order to protect our shores from the enemy. Anyway, he would return and we had to sit at a very large table and enlarge all the film he took to the size of a huge wall. Then, under a bright light, we would take a special brush and dot the areas that needed his attention."

Marion was a great worker there, she was well-liked, never staying out sick, always on time, and got along great with all the other working girls. She was an exemplary employee at work, and at home she was an exemplary daughter, resuming her motherly role as well.

Because of the vast age difference, she and Jimmie pretty much "adopted" Marion's little sister, Avis, who then was about 7 or 8, and her little brother, Bobbie, 5 or 6. It was Jimmie and Marion who took them to school and back, always having a treat in a brown paper bag waiting for each of them as they stood on the corner before walking them safely home. Avis recalls, to this day, that it was Marion and Jimmie who provided many of the "firsts" in her life. It was they who took her for her first pony ride, first circus, and first ice follies. It was Jimmie and Marion who would take them shopping for toys, all with Edie Mae's permission, of course. Yet, as one can see, Jimmie and Marion were actually parents before they were parents.

In the summer of '42, in between all of these happenings in her life, she was still playing baseball ... always baseball. Though still playing with *The Olympets*, she had joined another team: The Melly Club out of Everett, MA. It was during this time that she met a good third baseman by the name of Maddy English, who also hailed from Everett. (Maddy had actually made the 2nd best team, *The Gardenias*, in the tryouts back in 1938 in the Boston Garden, while Marion had made the top team, *The Olympets*.) Maddy had a rifle of an arm and covered third like no other. At any rate, this friendship would actually have a story attached to it a little later in life, when fate would come calling with "belles" on for Marion offering her a place to play on the now famous League: *The Racine Belles*.

However, a belle, like Marion, would not be a single one for long.

11

The 'Glory-ous' Proposal

Marion was unsettled to begin with when they arrived at Jimmie's mother's house. It was, as Marion would say, hotter than H-E-Double-Hockey-Sticks. It always seemed to be on her birthday: July the 30th. But, she was aware that it wasn't just the heat that was unsettling her stomach. She knew this was the day they were going to break the news to Veronica that they were planning to get married. (But, first a little background information):

The world was now at war with The Fuhrer and his Nazi ideology moving steadfastly into Europe and beyond at a furious pace. Jimmie, the young soldier, now felt the pressure to pick up his pace and set a date for their wedding before WW II would take him elsewhere, as it did for Marion's brothers. All of them (who were of age) were sent off to fight in different directions: Al to the Aleutian Islands off the coast of Alaska, Frank to the Coast Guard in Boston, and Arthur was drafted into the signal corps of the Army.

Also in early 1943, after completing his basic training, Jimmie was transferred to Westover Air Base in Springfield, Massachusetts where he was promoted to staff sergeant in the Air Corps. His superiors had told him that non-commissioned officers could bring their spouses and family to live with them on base. While Jimmie was at Westover, Marion would drive there—by herself—to visit him. They would stop by the USO post for a game of ping-pong "where I did beat him most of the time" or talk on the porch into the night with other married Air Corps couples. Soon, Jimmie thought, he and Marion would be just like them. And, with that in mind, he had decided the timing was right to make Marion his wife. Her birthday, he thought, would be the perfect day to propose.

He was certainly nervous on the inside, but … on the outside, he remained his characteristically calm and easygoing self. Their plan was perfect and he felt good about it … in a few short months, he would be a non-commissioned officer living with his wife on base. Even though they would have a very short engagement, and things appeared harried, all would be fine. (After all, remember, they had dated for almost 5 years now.) He would assure his mother that the timing was right. After the wedding, he and his bride-to-be would soon live on base together. All would go smoothly. Surely, his mother would understand that.

Jimmie and Marion had decided on their rings and the big date already. In fact, they had previously had them engraved with the wedding date: September 5, 1943. Jimmie's father, James Honeywell Rush, had picked the jewelry up on his way home from his job in the lab at the Dupont Paint factory in Boston. According to the 'proposal plan' they had conjured up together, his son would surprise his bride-to-be with the ring during supper. The surprise that ensued, however, was not a joyous one that one would characteristically expect to be the case when a couple announces their engagement.

Instead, it was one of sadness and bewilderment.

As Jimmie, Marion, Veronica, James, and Jimmie's aunt, Suzie, were finishing up around the supper table, just about to tackle the dishes, Jimmie presented the ring in its velvet box to his beloved-to-be. Jimmie's Dad and aunt's reaction was one of happiness. Veronica, on the other hand, was a different story. She was upset that they were rushing to get married in just *three short months*, and she **did not approve** and made it known.

Marion was heartbroken and crushed. She completely broke down and ran into another room in shock and disbelief. Jimmie, forever her protector, rushed in to comfort her, his arm around her shoulders. He told her it would all work out, and that they would soon be together as husband and wife living on Westover Air Base.

Marion calmed, as she believed this would be the case as well. But, she couldn't understand Veronica's cold reaction.

64-years later, a wiser—and not-so-naïve—Marion, realizes why:

"I suppose now, looking back on it, that Jimmie's mother thought maybe that I might be pregnant, but that could not have been further from the truth, as Jimmie and I, our relationship ... well, we were like a brother and sister."

On September 5th, 1943 that changed, as Jimmie Rush and Marion Schulze became: Mr. and Mrs. James Rush.

But, as usual in the game of Marion's life, she was thrown a curve ball. Even her wedding day—and subsequent honeymoon—would not go completely as planned, and she would need to summon her characteristic patience and 'positivity' if she was to become a player on this new team she was about to join.

Team Three:
The Rushes

12

September 5, 1943—The Most 'Glory-ous' Day of All

Walking down the long aisle of a church, all eyes transfixed on the bride, dressed in a beautiful, shimmering white wedding gown complete with an overflowing train of satin and chiffon while your young husband-to-be nervously awaits at the end of the aisle to meet, marry, and whisk you away to an exotic honeymoon—isn't this the way most young girls envision their wedding day?

In 1943, even the 26-year-old Marion Schulze did, although she would definitely not have minded foregoing the gown and train part, as frilly dresses were never her style and, as she now jokingly says, "I probably would have tripped on it down the aisle." (If she had had an aisle to walk down, that is.) But, it was her maid-of-honor, Gracie, (Al's wife) who had insisted she wear a gown for this number-one special day in her life. They had gone shopping together for it, even though Marion "felt like a worm out of the ocean" in a gown like that. But, since Gracie had wanted her to wear one, and knowing that it was she who had planned the details of the day, Marion gracefully complied for Gracie's sake, and the happy bride-to-be would soon have the traditional fantasy wedding of 1943 with gown and overflowing train trailing behind her as she walked down the aisle of a beautiful, but quaint, community Catholic church—The Most Blessed Sacrament in Wakefield, Massachusetts.

Unfortunately, what both Gracie and Marion had designed, devised, and envisioned for this special day would not go entirely according to plan, as Marion would not walk down an aisle of a church, all eyes gazing at her, and the train on her gown would soon give way to the express train to the Big Apple (not exactly the exotic honeymoon getaway). In fact, Jimmie and Marion's entire wedding experience might actually be viewed as a cross between episodes of *The Honeymooners* meets the *Out-of-Towners*. It was, however, the cross, that was exactly the problem, and what proved to be Marion's 'cross to bear' on her wedding day.

Religion, you see, is what cost her her "dream" wedding. Being a Protestant, Marion was not allowed to marry a man with a staunch Catholic upbringing before the cross in the eyes of the church, especially in the actual building. Marion and Jimmie, therefore, had to exchange their vows in what they called "The Priest's House" with no aisle to walk down, but dressed in her white gown, in spite of that fact on September 5th, 1943.

"It was a small ceremony on a beautiful day. Fr. Hartigan married us. Oh my Glory! Did Jimmie look handsome! He had on his Air Corps uniform with the stars and stripes. My wonderful sister-in-law Gracie was my maid of honor (as she was a Catholic and Marion's sisters were not) and Jimmie had a sergeant (also a Catholic) that was with him on the Air Base as his best man. Just the two of them, along with our parents, and Jimmie's aunt were present. I wasn't able to walk down the aisle in my nice white dress, as we were what you would call a "mixed marriage."

(This is an important point. As Marion could have legitimately held a grudge with the Catholic Church for not allowing her to actually marry in it, but, characteristically, Marion's personality would not allow this, and later in her marriage, she realized it would be for the good of their children for her to convert to Catholicism.)

True, the union of Marion and Jimmie was small and quiet, but the reception with all the Schulzes there, including little sister, Avis, and brother, Bobby, certainly was not. Some of her older brothers, however, could not be there as they were off fighting World War II in different corners of the globe.

"The reception," she recalls, "was in Maplewood Square (in Malden), a small hall with all our parents and friends there."

Though the partying for the newlyweds went on for hours and hours, Marion grew anxious. She knew they had to catch the train by 11:00 in order to make it to New York. Finally, they broke free from the relatives and her father drove them to South Station to catch the "*Midnight Express*" to the Big Apple.

"We had put a deposit for a nice room in New York City. When we arrived, however, there was "no room at the inn." The man standing at the shiny marble desk in the lobby told us we were too late ... 'We gave your room away to another couple,' he said. It was Labor Day weekend and rooms were scarce."

Thankfully, the concierge got these newlywed-out-of-towners another room in a different hotel. "It was a very nice suite, but we had to pay plenty for it."

Yet, that little glitch in their plans didn't ruin this happy couple's time. For one week, these greenhorn-honeymooners saw the sights of the Big Apple. One of their highlights was eating at an official New York automat named after the famous boxer in the 1920s Jack Dempsey, a.k.a. *The Manassa Mauler*. Jack Dempsey's Dine-O-Mat was a combination fast-food vending and cafeteria-style restaurant where ready-made meals are viewed through little windowed NY 'apartments' for a few coins or two. (Something that the easy-to-please palates of Jimmie and Marion thought was simply Dine-O-Mite!) Another of their honeymoon adventures included a mystery cab ride that the dapper Jimmie had spontaneously arranged to Belmont Racetrack. Marion cheerfully went along for the ride. "That's when my friend here,"she says as she lovingly points to her now-94-year-old spouse, "used to take care of the budget." (In their later years, betting on the ponies at the track at Rockingham Park in New Hampshire, an hour's ride from their home would be a hobby that this happy couple would also enjoy together—and everything they do now and did then, as you can see by now, is always linked in some way to the world of sports.)

But, two better sports could not be found the world over than Jimmie & Marion Rush, as they take everything in stride that comes their way, even a less than perfectly planned after-wedding getaway.

Yet, as they say, all good things come to an end even for the mild—and certainly not wild—ride these honeymooners from out-of-town were on as they viewed the bright lights of New York City for one whole week without a care in the world. When they returned home, however, they both had yet another surprise and cross to bear awaiting them—courtesy of Uncle Sam.

13

The Afterglow of Glory: The Newlyweds Return

One week of wedded bliss. That's all the newly wed Mr. and Mrs. James Rush had before the draft board and Uncle Sam called Jimmie to duty. The rosy glow on the blushing bride's cheeks didn't even have time to pale.

They had just returned home from their honeymoon in hopes of living out their plan to reside on Westover Air Base: that being Jimmie, the staff sergeant and non-commissioned officer able to have his new bride by his side.

"Well that soon changed. Jimmie was suddenly alerted he was being transferred to another Air Base in Bangor, Maine. He ended up being there for about a year and then he was later stationed for additional training in Manchester, New Hampshire."

While in Bangor, on some weekends, Marion would take a drive there with her brother, Arthur (before he was drafted) to visit Jimmie and Arthur's friend, Bucky Sheridan. As usual, Marion's best friend, her Dad, was always there for her and would let her take the family car, no questions asked.

But, little did Marion know what a short stay that would be. She received a call one night while staying at Veronica's house. (Veronica, at times, would put a cot up for Marion in the sewing room so that she could stay over while Jimmie was on leave.) That fateful call came from her very hesitant husband who had to break the news to his brand-new bride that he was being shipped out to England in the morning. (Because of his own athletic background and achievements while at Everett High School, and due to the basketball coaching position he held with the Collins Club, of which Marion was a member, Uncle Sam felt the best job for this man was to make him the physical education trainer for the pilots' home base in England. He was the man whose job it was to keep them in tip-top shape so that they would be physically fit to stay awake and strong enough to fight full throttle with the Germans.) Of course, at the time, he was unaware of his mission … all he knew was that he was going to England in the morning.

Marion, upon hearing this devastating news, immediately called her best friend in the world—her Dad—and asked him if it would be okay to take the family car, even though it was quite late at night. Of course, his reply to his little girl was YES—again with no questions asked, and she drove by herself on the 1-hour+ ride to Manchester, New Hampshire to see her new husband off to board the plane to England that World War II booked for him.

That left Marion, if you will, essentially a "newlywed widow," all alone, and feeling as if the marriage was somehow all just a big dream.

And it did feel exactly like that—a big dream—particularly when a dream-offer came her way—one so big, that under normal circumstances, she would have accepted and yelped with a very big whoop of "Oh, My Glory! And, then she would have jumped for joy.

Marion was at practice in the Garden with her teammates, throwing the ball around and running the bases. *The Olympets* were dwindling, but there was chatter amongst the girls about a new team being formed. Ralph Wheeler, who had been following the *Olympets* in the papers, had gotten in touch with Howie McHugh, their publicity agent, asking him to recommend his best talent. He was planning to form a national women's softball team that would play the stadiums that normally the men fighting overseas would fill. Howie had received Marion's name from Maddy English, whom Marion had been teammates with on the Melly Club of Everett, and who had played on the *Gardenias*, the second team to feed into the *Olympets* in the Garden. Howie had given Ralph Wheeler several names: Maddy English, Gabby Chiano, Mary Pratt, Pat Courtney, and … Marion 'Schulzie' Rush. He asked them if they wanted to join and play for the now-famous team called: *The Racine Belles!* But, there was a catch. If they accepted, they would have to leave right away for Wisconsin. Well, there was no way on God's green earth that Marion would leave Malden after just finding out her husband was being shipped off to England. "I could never have done that," she says, "it just would not have been right." (In Marion's mind, that would just have been selfish, and that is something she never is.)

The others accepted the offer. Maddy went on to Wisconsin (and also to later fame in the city of Everett's history, having a school named after her in that fair town). Marion chose a different path.

With ambivalence in her shaky but thankful voice echoing throughout the hallowed arena of the Boston Garden, but with confidence in her choice, she graciously turned down Howie and Ralph's offer, and the rest, as they say, is history.

(Had Marion said yes to Ralph and Howie's proposal, it could have been her life's softball-driven story portrayed by Madonna, Rosie O'Donnell, or Geena Davis in the movie *A League of Their Own*.)

Coincidentally, however, on *her* own is exactly what she was. After refusing to go out west to Wisconsin, she suddenly found herself exactly that—alone—without her husband, and yet living with her new in-laws. She knew she couldn't stay with Veronica and the Rushes any longer; it just would be too uncomfortable. So, the newly-one-week-married Marion Rush now moved back in with *her* parents and remaining siblings, suddenly feeling, once again, like Marion Schulze, except for the little gold wedding band on her hand that told her differently.

It was certainly a familiar feeling being back in her old house, but it was also very crowded. The small bedrooms now felt even smaller, as she once again shared a room with her little sister, Ruthie, who now wasn't so little anymore, and both needed to share clothes for work as well, and that meant fancy, hard-to-come-by nylons, not pantyhose. Nylons, you see, were very hard to come by, as the government rationed them. (The silk in them was used to make the parachutes that the paratroopers used in the war to jump out of the airplanes.) Anyway, Marion needed the few pair of nylons she did have to wear to work at the US Engineers Office, but Ruthie had a fancy for them herself, as well.

"We had to share the same room and only one bed. She was a stocky girl, and I was very skinny, so she took up most of the bed. She would pull a little sneak on me when I was at work and would use my nice, new pantyhose and then deny it, which made me mad, and I would hold them up to show her how much she enlarged them. She would try to hide them, but I caught her many, many times."

Another thing that Marion caught many, many times as a workingwoman while Jimmie was in England was baseball games at Fenway Park. You see, the U.S. Engineers office was located in Copley Square at the time, which was right near to this historic Boston landmark.

"Being a red-hot-Red-Sox baseball fan, I knew all the batting averages of most of the players that I liked. Well, the Red Sox announced they were going to have what was known as Ladies Day where all the ladies were able to go and see the games at no cost."

(This is the only time in her life that Marion actually pulled a "little sneak" of her own.)

"When there was a good team coming to play I had to think of a reason to see the game and get out of work, so I soon began to have a very bad headache, so I had to go home." (To home plate, was more like it, however.)

"I did not go home, as I ended up at Fenway Park to watch the Red Sox. I saw a lot of good players like Ted Williams, the "little professor" Dom DiMaggio, and many others that I really liked. Of course, I admired the whole Red Sox team, but Joe Cronin was my favorite one that I liked the best. Jerry Remy was one little player that came along and I followed his career. He was a very good second baseman and a good hitter until he got a very bad knee injury and he was out for a long time, but now he is still connected to the Red Sox, as their analysis person and he is tops in that field."

Playing the field, however, while her husband was away overseas for 3+ years, was something that the forever faithful, yet young and beautiful Marion Rush, would never do. She was a woman who took her sacred vows seriously, whether they were spoken in a church that wasn't even of her denomination, or whether they were spoken in the "priest's house." In fact, religion—the Catholic religion—actually played a role in how she would spend her nights while Jimmie was away serving his country. She got to be good friends with a couple of the ladies with whom she worked at the Engineers Office, who happened, also, to have spouses that World War II had taken to different parts of the world. On Friday's after work, they would all go bowling together. One co-worker, Dottie Palmer, was "half-Negro" and she and Marion became great friends. "A wonderful, wonderful, woman" she said. (Marion was and always has been 'color-blind' and would later choose Dottie to be godmother to one of her children. Remember, this was a time in history when prejudice towards African-Americans was at its heyday.)

But, all these ladies, including Dottie, played an important role in Marion's life while Jimmie was away, and not just on bowling-night-Friday's either.

"Each of us were married and our husbands were away in the service, so every Monday night, after we finished work, we would go over to the Mission Church in West Roxbury. They would have a novena on that night, and we would pray for the safety of our husbands. Father Mantle (no known relation to Mickey to date) gave beautiful, beautiful what'cha-ma-callits—'hominies' (notice the Marionism), I mean homilies, and we enjoyed every bit of it."

Yet, attending novenas and praying on Monday nights wasn't the end of the lengths to which Marion would go to prove just how serious and respectful she was of her new husband's family and faith. For that, she would heed the advice of her best friend—her Dad.

"My father advised me to become a Catholic, as he knew that when we had children when Jimmie came home, I would have to help them with catechism and schoolwork, so I did—I studied hard—became a Catholic, and made my first confirmation before Jimmie came home from the service."

And, some three-plus-years later, that is exactly what happened. Jimmie returned home to begin a new life together and resume where they left off on their one-week marriage in, what Jimmie thought of as *"This Old House."*

Translation: back with his parents.

14

How Do You Spell Glory?
G.I. J-I-M Comes H-O-M-E.

Ruthie was totally unaware who was at the door when the doorbell chimed.

It was a bitter-cold January day in 1946, and she certainly didn't feel like opening it up and letting a big blast of winter's frosty breath filter through the entire Eastern Avenue house. But, she did.

Standing on the stoop, waiting to reunite with the love of his life, was her good ol' faithful brother-in-law, Jimmie Rush, looking ever so dapper and dashing in his Air Corps uniform, all stars and stripes and patriotic-polished.

"Can I come in?" he said with his usual meek, but likeable smile, the twinkle in his blue eyes reflecting sunlight like an ice-covered pond. "Is she here? He pursed his fingers to his lips to shush Ruthie's expected exclamation.

"She's here," Ruthie said in hushed tones, "I'll get her for ya"

"Maaarrrrrionnnnnn!" the not-so-genteel Ruthie yelled. "Get down here, right away!" (Ruthie could always sound a little rough on the edges, but she had a heart of pure silk-spun gold.)

Marion came rushing down the stairs.

Well, when she finally came eye-to-eye with her beloved husband who had been overseas for nearly four years, the response that Ruthie witnessed was totally unexpected, and yet, typical for the type of relationship that Jimmie and Marion had.

"Jimmie, you old dog, you!" exclaimed Marion. Then, she did what every new bride who reunites with her long-lost GI husband would do—*she punched him in the arm*! (And, *he did likewise to her!*) That was their very own signature term of endearment.

(Of course, a hug and a kiss ensued. But, hey, nothin' says lovin' like a light punch in the side of the arm, right? That was Jimmie and Marion's unique way of showing affection to one another. Ruthie was, of course, astonished by the way they greeted each other and *never, ever* forgot this heartwarming and comical reunion story. In fact, 50 years later, when Jimmie and Marion celebrated their golden anniversary, Ruthie wrote of witnessing this very special encounter.)

But, now that GI Jim was home, where on earth would these newlyweds rekindle their relationship, where on earth would they live? These were all questions that swirled through Marion's brain like bees around a hive.

Reality hit home for the two of them. After the war, apartments were extremely scarce due to the influx of GIs returning to the states who were all looking to set-up housekeeping with rekindled romances and the heated desire to start their own families.

The one and only answer for Jimmie and Marion was for them to move in with Veronica and Jimmie's father, James. "We stayed there from January 1946 until August 1948 and it was very hard. We were mostly in our one bedroom upstairs."

In the meantime, Marion decided it was time to leave her job at the U.S. Engineers Office now that Jimmie was home from the war. The many friends she made there wanted to give her a big send-off party, but that was just not Marion's style. So, they took up a collection and brought their gift to her house: a beautiful green, marble clock with gold wings on it, representing the Air Corps. Then, without much fanfare, they wished her well in her new life.

And, a new life is exactly what Marion got. The hands on the old biological clock were ticking, and they told her it was time for a change—in nine months!

15

The Glory of Life

Marion knew her body was changing, the rapidly growing softball-sized bump in her normally flat-and-fit-from-sports stomach told her so. She also knew she needed to see a doctor because she was, indeed, with child. That meant the extremely modest Marion had to face that fact—and the consequences of—the facts of life.

"I was so scared, as I never went to a doctor before and had to remove all my clothes to be examined. At that time, a doctor did not seem to mind if you put on a lot of weight, and boy, I sure did pile it on!"

Perhaps that was all there was for Marion to do but eat, eat, and eat while trying to live quietly with her in laws, trying ever so carefully not to make too much noise or commotion in her one bedroom hideaway while Jimmie was working during the day at Kyanize Paint.

But, noise certainly was made nine months later.

"I had to wake Jimmie up early one morning. I had one little suitcase ready because I had those pains you get when you're going to deliver. Jimmie was calm as ever, but my water broke in the car on the way to Malden Hospital. In those days, the father wasn't allowed in the delivery room, so they sent Jimmie home to wait. I remember they gave me something to put me to sleep. The last thing I remember hearing was the nurse saying: 'I hear two heartbeats' and then … I passed out."

When Marion awoke, she was the mother of a new baby boy: little Jimmie, Jr., who was born on February 14th, 1947, weighing in at 10 lbs., 2 oz.

"Because he was such a big baby, and after I delivered the afterbirth, they had to come in with some kind of a whatcha-callit—lamp … some kind of a lamp to heal the incision. After I came home, Mae (Jimmie's aunt who also lived at Veronica's) did that for me. It wasn't a flashlight … it was some kind of a lamp that they put on the 'decision' down below." (Did you notice the sweet little Marionism again?)

Actually, however, it was more like up above in the second floor apartment where the action was.

For the long months after 'little Jimmie' was born, Marion tried to keep him as occupied and quiet as possible.

"We stayed mostly in our one bedroom upstairs and I played with him on a little balcony that was off of our bedroom for him to get the sun—until it was time to pick up his father at the train station at Boston Garden returning from work at Kyanize Paint. I mostly stayed in our one bedroom while he was growing up."

(Imagine trying to entertain a baby in crowded quarters like that! But, guess there wasn't much to do up there, as, sure enough, another baby was soon on its way.)

"Finally, after living with Jimmie's parents for 18 months, when I knew for sure another baby was on its way, I insisted to my husband that we had to move into our own place. Jimmie didn't care too much for that idea, as he was home with his parents. But, I found a nice real estate man and he had just listed a beautiful two-family home. It was August 1948. Anyway, he arranged for my husband and I to see the house. Well, after touring it, we bought it. It was perfect … right across the street was a—***ballpark!*** In addition, it was handy to church, handy to school, and that's where we started our own home."

Then the Rush family tree began to grow a few more branches: a beautiful baby girl, Patricia Ann Rush, was born in 1948, and a few years later in 1952, little Edmund Francis (named after Jimmie's twin who had died choking on a bean as an infant) entered the modest but comfortable home located across the street from a ballpark, and into the arms—and gloves—of two sports-minded to a fever pitch, loving and caring parents.

And, then came the downstairs relatives …

16

The 'Glory-ous' Theory of Relativity

The theory is that what goes around comes around, particularly when it comes to how you treat others—especially your relatives.

And, when you own a two-family house, as Marion would find out, it sure comes in handy for those family members who need a helping hand in times of need, and whose helping hands, in turn, later return the favor. History would repeat itself, as follows:

Little did Veronica Rush know that one day, her daughter-in-law (that she really wasn't that warm and fuzzy to or caring of) would ultimately help her out the way she herself did for her own relatives—that being taking them in to live with her when they were down and out. In fact, in the early years, Veronica practically ran a hotel out of her house, taking in her sisters, a brother (and his wife and family). (This gets a little confusing with all the relatives' names, so you'll have to pay close attention.)

When Jimmie was a little boy, Veronica's sister, Mary Ellen (Mae) lived with them for years. Mae never married and was "awfully good to Jimmie." Veronica had another sister, Susie, whom Veronica also took in when Susie's husband passed away. Later on, Jimmie's mother allowed her brother, John, to come and live with Jimmie, James, and herself. John "liked his tea" but Veronica gave him a home nonetheless. It was really getting crowded in Jimmie's house, yet she took in Gertrude (another sister) and her husband ("a brilliant man"), who were both from Rhode Island. It was a full house, indeed! One has to give Veronica her due, however, as she was always willing to help family in need.

Later in life, it was her husband who needed the care, however. One day, as he was walking home from the Melrose Depot after work and after also stopping for two bags of groceries, he collapsed. It was a stroke, and it was Veronica who lovingly cared for him at home for years until he passed away. As Marion points out: "She was wonderful to him."

When it came to who was wonderful to Veronica, however, it was her not-so-favorite daughter-in-law. Marion gave Veronica a helping hand when she needed it, and the two-family house, across from the ballpark, that Jimmie and Marion purchased provided her mother-in-law the much-needed shelter and caring for many years that not only she, but her other relatives, as well, needed. Before coming to live with them, it was Jimmie and Marion who would get Veronica's groceries for her when needed, requiring them to take two bus changes to the store and back (when her car stood idle in her garage). And, it was Jimmie and Marion who would drive her to appointments, Sunday drives, and the like. The other in-laws were well taken care of as well. In fact, one could say the "hotel" that Veronica herself ran for her family members had now moved to Granite Street, complete with the metaphorical revolving door.

You see, after Veronica's husband died, and after Gertrude's husband had passed away, Veronica became Jimmie and Marion's downstairs tenant. Then, Mae joined her. Next, came Veronica's brother, Alexander, whom the family called "Nan."

"When Nan died, sure enough, Susie came along because she used to live with her son, Georgie, and his wife, (are you ready for this?) Georgianna. We called her Gigi. Well, Susie disliked Gigi, as Gigi had some problems or issues it seemed. Well, Gigi ended up being put away and that left Georgie trying to find a home for his mother, and that's how Susie ended up living downstairs from us."

As time went on, Veronica passed away, which was devastating to Jimmie. "She had what we thought was the flu. We called the doctor and next the ambulance, and they took her off to the Malden Hospital, but it was too late. She was D.O.A. It was quite a blow to Jimmie." Six months later, Mae, passed away. Now, that left Susie alone downstairs.

"One morning, Susie fell on the floor and broke her hip. She had thought she had seen mice, but there were no mice. Georgie, her son, thought it was time to place her. So he placed her into the Dexter House (a sort of nursing home) in Malden. Georgie couldn't come and visit her much because he had two sons of his own, so Jimmie and I went several days a week to visit with Susie. Susie also had another son who was her favorite, Leo. Leo traveled back and forth to South America. He had a woman down there. When Susie died, we thought at least half the money Susie had would go to Georgie, but it didn't … she gave it all to Leo."

They say that good deeds are rewarded, but as you can see by this story, for Jimmie and Marion, the monetary rewards from the relatives they helped just did not come their way. Financial assistance and inheritances from all these women whom they helped went to others. Mae, who inherited a lot of money from an uncle of hers, left everything to Susie. She only gave Jimmie an E-bond from the war that Marion says she still has to this day. But, that was all Jimmie got from Mae. As for an inheritance from Veronica (Jimmie's mother) for all her son and daughter-in-law did for her … well, she gave a small amount to Jimmie and the rest she sent to the priests in her parish."

However, Jimmie and Marion didn't do these good deeds for the money, they did it for the love, the love that would also be returned to them in the not too distant future of their golden years—and it would come from their own family and downstairs relatives.

But, first we must go backwards a bit by a few decades before we can get to that future.

17

The Glory of Motherhood and the Mundane

As any mother can attest to, motherhood is a full-time job. It is one that requires wearing many different hats: mother, nurse, cook, waitress, chambermaid, house-keeper, event planner, friend, and, especially in the Rush family—coach. It's a thankless job of mundane tasks like cooking, cleaning, and ironing, all while changing diapers, wiping runny noses, and giving baths to little "athletes" with mud-soaked skin and bloody shins. And, all this is done while being perpetually tired from sleepless nights with crying infants, or nursing sick kids back to health from blustery New England flu-ridden winters. However, for most mothers, the real sleep deprivation culminates throughout the worrisome teen-aged years, and that is a fact that is true of mothers everywhere.

Fortunately, in the early years of the Rush children's lives, Marion, was a stay-at-home Mom. However, being a mother in the early 1950s without the luxury and convenience of products like Pampers, dishwashers (mothers back then had to hand-wash and sterilize diapers and bottles) or other modern-day appliances like washers and dryers (they had wringer-type washing machines with outdoor clotheslines for drying) and quick-as-a-beep-beep microwave, ready-made meals—it simply just wasn't as easy being a mother then as it is today.

For Marion Rush, however, even then she managed all these tasks exceedingly well, almost as if she had one hand tied behind her back. Well, she might as well have, if you consider the fact that one always seemed to be in a baseball glove whenever she could find the time. But, this time, it wasn't when she was playing with the pros like the *Olympets*. No, no, no … now she was the coach of a different team: The Rushes. Her children: Jimmie Jr., Pat, and little Eddie became her new teammates—and oh how she taught them well!

Of course, it helped a lot to live across the street from a ballpark, which made it extra easy to squeeze in a lesson or two on how to hold the bat, swing, bunt, run the bases, or catch fly balls. She even invented a game she called "Rollies at the Bat" and every night after supper when they were little, the whole family would go across the street for a quick game. The way it worked was like this: The kids and Jimmie, Sr. would be stationed strategically in either the infield or the outfield. Marion would be at home plate. After she swung the ball with the bat, she would lie it down on the ground at home. Then the kids or Jimmie would try to catch it and throw it back to the plate. Most of the time, the ball rolls when it gets close to the bat and when it hits it, it usually pops up. If Marion didn't catch it, she would be out and whoever threw it would come to the plate to throw the next ball. And, so it went for many, many nights.

When the family wasn't in the mood for baseball, though, they'd all go out in the backyard for a game of hoop. But, first they actually needed one. That's when Marion came to the rescue. It was she who climbed a ladder and nailed a basket to their house in order for them to have a place to play, and, even though the house was located on a street named Granite Street, the backyard itself wasn't exactly made of it. It was a dirt yard, but somehow the family would play games of "*horse*" OR "21" until the cows came home. (Sounds a bit reminiscent of the days of the cow pasture of Eastern Avenue, doesn't it?)

Jimmie and Marion were always on hand to play catch or any kind of ball with their kids and friends. That's just how the Rushes were for years. The door to their house was always open for the neighborhood gang, just as long as one parent was home at all times. In the winter, or on rainy days, Marion would play games of monopoly, cards, or Scrabble, particularly with her daughter, Pat. She had a smart head for that sort of thing. Then, when the boys were in junior high school, she'd join right in with them and their friends for ping-pong tournaments in their cellar, where a table that Santa had bought years earlier was set-up.

Speaking of Santa, Christmas mornings at the Rush household was also something to behold. Truckloads of presents would be under the tree—unwrapped, as Santa was so busy out buying presents that there just wasn't time to wrap them up in pretty paper and bows. That's because Santa was busy running the household and working essentially two jobs.

Sure, Jimmie Sr. was working at Kyanize Paint in Everett, but it still wasn't enough money to run the house on one pay. That's when Marion decided it was time to get a job.

"It was right after our littlest son was in the second grade. I decided I wanted to get a part-time job, and I did with the W.C. Grant Company, mother's hours, so I could be home when the children were home from school. So, from 8:30 in the morning to 2:00 in the afternoon, I would have to dash home to make sure I was home for them and make supper for the family."

To top that off, on certain days, she would stop to pick up Veronica (this was before she lived downstairs). "She would watch me make supper, and boy, did it made me nervous."

Then, after the meal was eaten and the supper dishes were cleared, she would fly back to Grants to work the 5:00 P.M. to 9:00 P.M. shift. (Talk about a woman bringing home the bacon, frying it up in the pan, and working like a man!)

Sometimes, however, illness would befall the family, and Marion, again, would step in as Supermom to save the day.

"Eddie seemed to be hurt quite a bit, as he was very active and sort of a dare-devil as a son. Playing in the yard with his friends, one of them fell on his stomach and I had to take him to the hospital. This happened to Eddie himself several times. Once, he had appendicitis and had to be operated on at midnight. Jimmie Jr. had his share of troubles. He had a 'bronical' cough (notice the sweet little Marionism, again) real bad and had pneumonia at one time, so I had to watch over him. Patti, my ambitious highschooler had found work at two jobs until it caught up with her, and she came down with mononucleosis. After that, she had to settle down and only work one job."

Marion's work ethic was, likewise, like her daughter's. When she wasn't taking care of her sick children, she was working her way up the retail ladder at Grants. Marion started out there by putting tags in the back on merchandise, but before long she was placed in every department in the store until she knew each one of them inside and out. Then, she was promoted to the office and, later was given the distinction of being the first one to open the store in the morning and the last one to close it.

"The only department I didn't like working in was the pet department, as I didn't know too much about that, putting the goldfish in bags and all that. I did that to cover other ladies on their lunch hour. The department I enjoyed working in the best was sporting goods." (Gee, that's no surprise to us, is it?)

Yes, Marion did any job and *anything* she could think of to help with the family budget. Gone were the days when it was Jimmie who ran the household, as she managed more than just the checkbook. She was the one who was the disciplinarian with the children.

"In the beginning Jimmie thought I was not strict enough ... but I soon became the one to enforce the rules. They were all good kids, however ... a combination of both of us. I believe Jimmie got his wit from me and he was like us in that he was always talking sports. Patti became a workaholic like her grandfather.

Eddie was the youngest in the family. When the others were in school, Eddie and I became very close. We would take the train in to Boston to shop for bargains, especially in the winter. He loved seeing the *Enchanted Village* that the old *Jordan Marsh* store put on every Christmas. (This was an entire floor of the store set-up with miniature lighted houses, moving mannequins, and lights.) It was a sorry day when I had to send him off to school. He was also the one who was the most athletic in the family."

Typical of Marion, she points out each child's unique nature, not wanting to show any favoritism, even to this day:

"Patti used to take part in a lot of high school affairs. She was very sociable with a lot of friends. Eddie was the most athletic, as he played Little League baseball and then graduated to the Babe Ruth league. In high school, he was only a freshman and made the cross country team. Jimmie, Jr. also played Little League baseball, but he did not enthuse over it. He enjoyed playing hockey, and was always the goalie, as he could not skate very well. But he didn't need to skate when he played the game with his little brother in the long hallway in our house. Eddie would try to get the puck past Jimmie, the goalie, but once they broke my window in the living room, so they changed from playing with a real puck to a pair of folded up socks."

Another bit of mischief the boys got into was courtesy of Marion's good ol' buddy, Maddy English. As you recall, Maddy was Marion's teammate on the *Olympets*, who later went on to fame as the third baseman for *The Racine Belles*.

"I picked Maddy as Jimmie Jr's godmother, because Maddy was Catholic … and such a good friend. Well, Maddy had given Jimmie a pair of boxing gloves for his birthday. Well, Jimmie, Jr. and Eddie would go at it with those gloves when I would be at work. Finally, I had to put a stop to it, as they were really beating each other up pretty good. So, I had to think of something. Well, I found a special place in the attic for those gloves, and that put an end to that, and the problem was solved."

However, when the Rush kids hit their teen years, the problems of parenting, along with the problems of aging parents and relatives grew too—and those were not such an easy fix for Jimmie and Marion.

18

The "Glory-ous" Times They Are a Changin'

The fabulous '50s ended as just that for the Rush family: Marion & Jimmie's children were now all in school, even their youngest son, Eddie and they had their beautiful two-family home across the street from Trafton Park. They were living within their budget, thanks to Marion going to work and, though times were tight, she kept her eyes carefully monitoring the checkbook to the bills. Even their family itself was cohesively bonding with the Schulzes, as Marion's youngest sister, Avis married a handsome young Scotsman, named Don (also known as Uncle Mac to the family) in 1957. Don had served in the Korean War, as well as Marion's younger brother, Bobbie. However, as Marion puts it, "Bobbie was never the same again." The family story goes like this: as a paratrooper over there, he contracted malaria and, upon his return, he never did quite reconnect with his Schulze family roots.

Jimmie Sr., however, was rooting his own way into the Schulze family hearts. He frequently went with Marion to her father's house to play whist with him on many an afternoon and was also a good friend to his other brother-in-law, Al, and his wonderful wife, Gracie. They happened to have a son (Donnie) and a daughter (Donna) who were the same ages as Jimmie Jr. and Patricia. Marion often went shopping and bowling with Gracie and all the kids.

It just appeared that both the Rushes and the Schulzes were all one happy family. This was particularly the case during holidays like Memorial Day or the 4th of July when all the Schulze and Rush clans would get together for fun times at family cookouts, either at Edie Mae's, Avis and her new husband, Don's, or in the case of the 4th of July, at Jimmie & Marion's, across from Trafton park. That's where all the festivities on the fourth took place like the Little Miss Maplewood beauty contest, doll-carriage contests, and the three-legged/cross-country running races.

Indeed, all things for the Rushes and the Schulzes seemed to be running quite smoothly. But, like so many other families, they, too, were unaware of the up-and-coming troubling times that the shadow of the '60s would cast on their happiness just over the hill on the horizon. This would be an era eerily characterized by the famous Bob Dylan lyrics in the song: *The Times They Are A-Changin'*.

The change came in many forms: change in children, change in parents. Some change came creeping in slowly and softly, and other changes came drastically without warning.

Luckily, for the Rushes, softball and sports was always a way to cushion the blows or to help them cope, just like their mother taught them it would. Marion, however, was characteristically the one to catch them all in bad times, and with three teen-agers in the household, one never knew quite what to expect.

"I worried quite a bit about them getting into trouble, like some of their other friends." (Remember, it was the days of the "hippie" in the 1960s, and drinking and drug use was rampant nationwide—but, the nation didn't have a mother like Marion to lay down the law.)

"They had rules and regulations to follow, and for quite a while the curfew was 11:00 P.M. for all of them."

Of course, for the Rush teen-agers, 11 P.M. was an easy curfew, as their softball games were well over by that time. Pat was playing for the St. Joseph's league in high school. Marion even served as assistant coach on that league for a short time—until that is when the other coach wanted to place the best player on the team way, way out in the outfield. (You would think the coach would have listened to a former *Boston Olympet,* but the woman didn't.) That's when Marion decided to call it a day on coaching the St. Joe's team.

Eddie, in the meantime was busy in his high school sports, playing on the hockey team, running indoor-outdoor track, and also running with the distinction of being the cross-country captain. (He recalls hockey practices at 5 and 6 o'clock in the morning held at the outside rink at Breakheart Reservation in Wakefield, MA or the MDC rink in Medford. There, he would look out, skating on the ice to see only two people off to the sides, patiently watching, yet shivering off the cold in worn, woolen, winter coats. Those two people: Jimmie and Marion Rush. They would also be the only parents willing to get up that early to drive any and all of his team member friends to practice, as well.)

They did the same for Jimmie, Jr., when he played pond hockey, but for Jimmie, Jr., he was more of an inside sports enthusiast, an avid collector of sports memorabilia (cards, sports figurines, and magazines) who could talk sportsology better than anyone.

Sports also kept Jimmie Sr. busy, as well in those days, as he coached Malden Little Leaguers. He was also appointed as a scout in the 1960s for the Cincinnati Reds, and would travel around the metro-Boston area, Maine, Cape Cod, Rhode Island, and central Massachusetts area to look for talent in semi-professional leagues throughout the area.

Summer vacations for the Rushes included pretty much the same sports-themed outings that included day trips to Portland, Maine; Manchester, New Hampshire; or to Phillips Academy in Andover, MA where they would watch The New England Patriots practice. On occasion, they would stop along the way to give the kids some fun and good times at indoor sports games in the arcades of various beaches along the New England coastline.

But, along with the good times, came the bad, as the times they were a-changin' for the Rushes, they just didn't know it, particularly when it came to Marion's father, Arthur Schulze.

The special bond between a daughter and her Dad was never more evident than in Marion and Arthur's case; she absolutely idolized her father. He was her rock in hard times and the person she turned to for advice during them. He taught her the important things in life, like how to balance household budgets and checkbooks, the importance of a good work ethic, and how the love and diligence in tending to one's garden in life yields not only the fruits of one's labor, but also some pretty tasty tomatoes right off the vine. But, most of all, what Arthur taught her was to be independent. Thanks to him, she gained the confidence and positive outlook that a woman raising a family in the 1960s needed in order to cope with the changing decade and issues of the time. She essentially became not only the primary disciplinarian to her teen-aged children, but also the "handyman" around the house, fixing every electrical problem, plumbing issue, or anything else that went wrong with the house on Granite Street by the park.

Unfortunately, the one thing that Marion could not fix was a broken heart, and that occurred in the tumultuous 60s for a number of reasons—the first being the literal breakdown of her father's heart that to her mysteriously failed without a clue.

"He took sick all of a sudden, totally out of the blue. My father went into the hospital because he had stomach pains and other discomforts. He was admitted to the hospital for a gallbladder operation. They had to put him in an oxygen tent because he couldn't breathe. During that night after the operation, my father took a bad turn. He died that night. We had a huge wake for him, as he was a very, very popular man, and he was buried in Puritan Lawn in Peabody. (Oddly enough, this is a cemetery that has a sign out on one of the busiest highways in the state: Route 1, where traffic whizzes by faster than one can read the billboard that states: "Visit the Park"—how à propos.)

At any rate, Arthur's death came as a total blow to the entire family. But, what was even more troubling to Marion was the statement the family physician made to Edie Mae.

"I heard him say to my mother, 'You know, I never knew Arthur had a heart condition.'" This was a totally puzzling comment, as even Marion knew her father was on Digitalis, a commonly known and prescribed medication for exactly that—a heart condition!

Nonetheless, the Schulze family said nothing and carried on, albeit in a zombie-like state for weeks that, for Marion, turned into months. She was utterly devastated by his death. Marion's little sister, Avis, tells how she never saw her big sister shed as much as a tear before their father's passing—and then the floodgates opened. Marion's heart was, likewise, broken and bruised. Thank goodness she at least had her husband and family's support to help her through this crushing ordeal.

The cruel '60s, however, continued to bring some unwelcome changes to Marion's otherwise happy life. With the advancing age of other family members, the foreboding fog of other losses haltingly and hauntingly crept into the decade. Veronica's death affected Jimmie in much the same devastating manner that Arthur's passing anguished Marion. The dual losses of Jimmie's aunts Mae and Suzie, whom you remember lived downstairs from Jimmie and Marion, also took its toll on the family. None, however, was as angst provoking and shocking as the death of Marion's beloved brother, Al.

An avid golfer in the family, Al would oftentimes take time out of work at the gas company to teach the game to his nephews (one of them Marion's youngest son, Eddie).

"Al had quite a bad time. It got to the point where he had to give up his golf because the ol' heart was giving out on him. The doctor decided to put him into the Mass. General Hospital. Day-by-day, he got worse, and I went over to see him, even though they didn't want me to go. I couldn't get over the change that came over him. Within the next week or two, he took a battle for the worst and he died. Gracie, his wife, was devastated. He was only in his early 60s, an absolutely wonderful brother."

Though Al's death was the pinnacle blow to Marion in these changing times, little did she know that Uncle Sam was about to give her yet something else to worry about. The country was in the throes of civil rights and riots, flower-power hippies, and the Vietnam War loomed above it all. Marion knew her oldest son was just the right age to be drafted. Jimmie Jr., at 19, also knew his number would be called soon if he didn't enlist, so that is exactly what he did. Coincidentally, he, like his father, joined the Air Force. The decision turned the Rush household upside down. As any mother of that era could attest to, the likelihood of a son that age going to Vietnam and coming home in a body bag was as high as a single digit draft number. Not every mother, however, would get up every morning at 5:00 A.M. for the 13 months that her son was over there in that war's hell hole, and faithfully write to her boy. Her youngest son, Eddie, recalls: "When I would get out of bed, I'd walk into the kitchen, all bleary-eyed to the smell of coffee brewing on the stove and breakfast cooking, but lo' and behold, there would be my mother sitting at the kitchen table every single, solitary morning, writing a letter to my brother."

Thankfully, due to all that loving correspondence, along with her heart-felt prayers, God was good to Marion. Jimmie, Jr. returned home in one piece back into the arms of his loving mother and father—and the Rush household became whole again. Life would be better now, back on the other side of the world where the '70s held the promise of a new decade for health and happiness.

19

The Glory Decades (1970–1980s)

With the tumultuous '60s now behind them, the children of Jimmie and Marion (even Jimmie Jr. home from Vietnam) essentially spent the mid to late 1970s as their growing years, living life pretty much as depicted on *That '70s Show*—out late, having a few laughs with buddies, working hard at various jobs (Patricia at two of them), all while struggling to find their way in the world. As for Marion, it was more like *The Golden Girls* meet *I Love Lucy* (with Jimmie resembling more of Fred Mertz than Ricky Ricardo. Allow me to 'esplain.'):

You see, by the time Marion turned 62-years-old, it was 1979. Jimmie had retired from Kyanize Paint where he had diligently worked for the past 43 years. He was hoping his wife would join him to enjoy their golden years together. (With his silver-fox hair, good looks, and easy-going manner to go along with whatever Marion wanted, Fred Mertz makes a good comparison.) She, however, was not ready to ultimately make that full-time commitment, instead choosing to semi-retire from the last paying job she worked at: Brudnick's.

Brudnick's was a factory, complete with conveyor belts where candy bars, cigarettes, or other novelty items were packed by women (before machinery took these jobs away from them.) Anyway, the bosses gave Marion the option of packing cigarettes or candy—she chose the candy (partly because she never liked cigarettes, never smoked, and partly because some of those paper-wrapped gum-packs came with baseball cards in them.) Sometimes the conveyor belt would go really, really fast, making it very difficult to keep up with the packaging process. (As one can imagine, this is where the *I Love Lucy* part comes into play!) (Actually, I am only joking, as Marion was a terrific worker who, once again, *Rush*ed to do her job better than anyone else.) They hated to even see her semi-retire.

But, it was time for that compromise for other reasons. Since her father's death, Edie Mae was now a widow, which meant that with Marion semi-retired, she had more time to care for and take her mother out shopping or to run errands and appointments, along, that is, with her little sister, Avis. (Avis pretty much became Edie Mae's caretaker after Arthur passed away. She and her husband, Don, were always there for her, letting her stay at their beautiful home with them for holidays, weekends, or other special events.) Otherwise, Edie Mae lived—and I do mean lived—in Malden's elderly housing apartments, enjoying all the senior citizen activities there such as Bingo, and, in particular—the dances. "We all tried to look after her, as she was alone … we all tried."

Semi-retirement also gave Marion and Jimmie the time and the desire to drive. And drive they did, both near and far to reconnect with friends and family. They would take long drives to Foxboro, MA to visit Jimmie's Everett High sports buddies, Lou Polansky and his wife, Lee, or to North Andover to see another old pal, Donny Drew, and his spouse. They also spent many a day and night with Marion's younger sister, Ruthie and her husband, Arthur, playing the ponies at Rockingham Park, the dogs at Seabrook, NH, or to see the trotters at the Rochester Fair where they enjoyed the Rush equivalent of the four basic food groups: a hot dog, burger, fries, and an ice cream. They also ate more dogs than they could bet on at Seabrook and had many of the same at the hundreds of fantastic family cookouts during this time in their lives at little sister, Avis' showplace of a home in Stoneham, Massachusetts. Summer was not complete back then without Avis' famous corn-on-the-cob, complemented by backyard bocce, badminton, and horseshoe tournaments all followed by a rousing game of Pass-the-Ace (where everyone plays a one-card game for pennies and where the money in the pot doesn't matter, but the fun sure does!)

Yes, good times and happiness abounded in these two decades for Marion and Jimmie.

"It was the best when our health was pretty good and we were able to do our own shopping and take a few automobile rides, stop, and get something to eat to take home." It was also the time in their children's lives when they searched and found exactly that too—happiness.

In the 1970s, their daughter Patricia, was living in their downstairs apartment while she worked at Harvard Medical as a secretary. In 1979, she later laid a bombshell on her parents, as she announced to them that she was moving to Florida. She decided to take a leap of faith and a chance on finding a new life, moving from downstairs beneath her parents to a state where she didn't know a soul. It later proved to be the best thing that ever happened to her, as she ended up finding her true love there, a man by the name of Richard, whom she met while working together for the Florida Power & Light Company. Nonetheless, the news was upsetting to Jimmie and Marion. As usual, however, they accepted her decision with happiness in their heart for her, but that also left them with a downstairs apartment that needed to be filled.

In the meantime, their oldest son, Jimmie, met the love of his life, Kathy, an Irish girl who hailed from Lawrence, MA and was by his side when he was injured and hospitalized after being sideswiped by a fire truck while on their way to an emergency call. By the fall of 1977, they were married and living in an apartment in Melrose. A year later, Marion and Jimmie were blessed with their first grandchild, Kelly, a bouncing blonde-haired beautiful little girl. With the downstairs apartment at Nana and Grampy's house now vacant, Kelly could now move in below them. Jimmie and Marion, the proud new grandparents were reveling in being just that, as evidenced by the bumper sticker on their car that read: "Ask us about Kelly." For two whole years, she was the apple of their eye until the arrival of their next little granddaughter, Kara, another beautiful blonde-haired baby, the second child of Jimmie Jr. and his wife, Kathy. They were equally enthralled with this new addition to their family.

In 1979, their youngest son, Eddie, married *his* one true love, Denise, another Lawrence girl of French-Canadian descent who also happened to be a friend of Kathy's, and who actually met the youngest dapper Rush boy at the wedding of Jimmie Jr. and his bride.) Eddie and Denise settled in southern NH and had two wonderful children of their own: a beautiful brunette baby girl, Lauren, with eyes as big and brown as her Nana's softball-sized ones, and a few years later, the first and only grandson of Jimmie and Marion's, Scott, a sweet blonde-haired baby boy. (Scott represents the hope of carrying on the Rush name, as Jimmie Sr., you might recall, is an only child and the lineage would otherwise end.)

The end of the line for Marion as far as her working years came by the time she reached 65-years-old.

"My body seemed to tell me I was tired and to slow down."

So, with that, Marion decided to call it quits and completely retire from her job at Brudnick's. Thankfully, she had her grandchildren to help her through that transition, between babysitting and picking up Kelly and Kara from school, and making all of them sweaters and afghans.

"After retiring, I had to find or do a happy hobby to keep my brain working. With that in mind, I started making afghans for all my grandchildren, relatives' grandchildren, and friends. I was known as the "afagan" queen (notice again the sweet 'Nana-ism' now, as we call it.) I started making little sweaters and mittens also. In my leisure time, in addition, I was also a very devoted Red Sox fan."

True it is … sports have always helped Marion cope. But, the amazing influence of sports in her life and outlook on life was never more strikingly evident than in her retirement. That is because between the Red Sox, Patriots, and college basketball, Marion and Jimmie could be found on any given day in their modest living room, sitting in their assigned seats—she in her recliner (sometimes with ears plugged into the radio, listening to another game while simultaneously crocheting an afghan, sweater, or mitten set), with Jimmie on the orange and brown plaid couch, watching every game they could. And, there you have it: New England's #1 sports fans, watching the game of life from their cushioned grandstands, experiencing the true meaning of being a good sport, knowing full well that sometimes you win one and sometimes you lose, but being proud of the team's effort nonetheless.

For Marion, however, she is even more proud of her team. During their retirement years, they had plenty of time to watch their children become parents, and watch their grandkids grow and learn. Marion and Jimmie, now affectionately known as Nana and Grampy, were always there to babysit, kiss a boo-boo, or help take care of their downstairs grandchildren whenever sickness came-a-callin'. Soon, however, within these golden years, the circle of life, as so often happens, started to move in the opposite direction and, in Jimmie and Marion's case, the health concerns that loomed overhead rained down on them from the gray clouds that were barely visible over the horizon.

20

The Glory of the Golden Years?

It began with Grampy.

Before his luck regarding his health took a backwards horseshoe turn in 1984, both he and Marion were two extremely healthy specimens of human beings who totally defied every bit of medical logic and advice that 20th century doctors could dispense. Their diet consisted mostly of hot dogs, fries, burgers, fried clams (from Woodman's in Ipswich, MA) doughnuts, ice cream, and cut-up tomatoes. They never saw a doctor, as Marion's "little yellow pill" was the cure-all for every cold and flu they ever caught. They never had their cholesterol checked, exercised (other than walking to the betting window at the track or down the flea market aisles of Revere and New Hampshire), and Marion never had a mammogram, Pap smear, or saw a gynecologist on a regular basis. They just took life as it came, never worrying—and they still do!

Yes, Grampy's heart attack struck without warning right before the birth of his third granddaughter, Lauren, in 1984. He didn't feel quite right and slumped to the floor. His daughter-in-law, Kathy, married to Jimmie Jr., (who luckily lived downstairs—and still does) came rushing up and immediately called 911. Thankfully, it was in time. After taking him by ambulance to the Melrose-Wakefield Hospital and, after running several tests, they determined it was a heart attack. The one good thing that came out of this episode was that Jimmie and Marion now had a family physician, Dr. Berg. (They picked him because he loves to talk Red Sox and other sports talk.) But, the long and the short of it was that Jimmie was now and forever to carry nitroglycerin tablets on his person wherever he went—just in case.

But, even a heart attack couldn't stop the Rovin' Rushes. After his recuperative period (and especially in the early '90s) Nana and Grampy would travel for miles in their brand new, Rush-red, Oldsmobile Cutlass Supreme, visiting relatives, long-distance friends, or stopping by their son, Eddie's house, who lived in New Hampshire for a visit with his wife and their children, Lauren and Scotty.

Sometimes they would even bring Edie Mae with them for a treat, and at other times, little sister Ruthie and her new husband, Arthur. It was during these years that they became snowbirds, flying to Florida for a month to escape a New England winter to visit their daughter Patricia, enjoying every minute with her and her then boyfriend, Richard. They enjoyed going to flea markets, Bingo games, Jai-Lai, or just playing cards and board games with their daughter and Gracie (another snowbird visitor), or simply watching the boats go by from the intercoastal canal penthouse condominium that Richard owned. When back at home in New England, however, they spent many weekends visiting their son, Eddie and his wife and children, always bringing a box of Dunkin' Munchkins along for their Lauren and Scotty or some of Nana's world famous brownies, and … on special holidays … Nana's world-renowned Lemon Meringue Pie. (Trust me, no one but no one makes lemon meringue pie like Marion Rush. It is a pic-ture-perfect "pie-a-cious" creation that looks like it could win the blue ribbon prize at the Pillsbury Bake-Off—and it tastes it too!)

Yes, those were the days! By the time the 1990s rolled around, Eddie and his wife had purchased a backyard pool, and Nana and Grampy would visit some-times twice a weekend, joining in with Denise's parents, for a couple of lazy after-noons of watching the kids swim and chatting it up around the deck. Later, when the sun went down, they would all pile into Eddie's silver and wood-striped Dodge Caravan to find a nice place to eat that offered up either fried clams or hot dogs. One memorable visit was when the whole clan piled into the van and went for a beautiful Sunday drive to visit the LaSalette Shrine in Ipswich, Massachu-setts. The grandparents sang songs and laughed all the way home. There was always something fun to do on the weekends when Nana and Grampy came up to New Hampshire for a visit.

Time was passing by quickly, however, and, in 1993, would you believe it? Jimmie and Marion Rush celebrated 50 years of marriage! The big party took place at their home across from the park, downstairs, in the home of their son, Jimmie Jr., Kathy, and their grandchildren, Kelly and Kara Rush. It was an abso-lutely beautiful affair with a house full of food, family, and some names from the past: Jimmie and Marion's friends (Maddy English from Marion's Olympet days and Donny Drew and Lou Polansky from Jimmie's Everett High baseball and basketball heydays). Everyone came from near and far to honor this wonderful couple on their special occasion. Their recently married daughter, Pat, and her new husband, Richard, flew all the way from Pompano Beach, Florida to the sur-prise and delight of her mother and father. The event was a team effort put together by all their children and family. It was spectacular! Jimmie and Marion were especially happy to share their 50 years of marriage and memories in their own abode.

The home on Granite Street, however, wouldn't be theirs for long. Both Jimmie and Marion knew that father-time was creeping up on them in some unkind ways, and that meant the time had come for them to think about their future, and do what was best for them with oncoming health concerns heading their way. That is when they made the decision to sell their home across from the park to Jimmie Jr. and Kathy. It turned out to be a very wise decision, as all the good deeds they did for the "downstairs relatives" like Veronica, May, Susie, and Nan would come full circle. Jimmie Jr. and his wife, Kathy, the new downstairs owners, would now become Jimmie and Marion's primary caregivers as they approached the very golden years of age 80 and beyond.

21

There's No "C" in Glory

Marion celebrated her 80th birthday in a most unusual way—on an operating room table!

It was 1997. She had been having some very severe stomach pains with vomiting episodes, and, once again, a trip to the Melrose-Wakefield Hospital yielded more tests ordered by Dr. Berg to diagnose the source of the problem. Marion braced herself to have "the broomstick" as she called it (also known in the medical world as a colonoscopy) to determine just what was happening "down there."

Well, the first diagnosis that came back was that Marion was having a bout of diverticulitis. After days of further testing and more "broomsticks up the backside," as Marion would say, it was determined that it was far more serious than that. The beloved matriarch of our family had the one diagnosis that no one in this world of ours ever wants to hear—CANCER. Yes, the Big-C, colon cancer to be exact, attacked the sweetest and most endearing gentle soul of a woman. How could this nasty, ugly disease happen to someone so lovely, wonderful, and caring?

But … it did—and it needed to come out.

So, on her 80th birthday, July 30th, 1997, Marion spent this memorable milestone on the operating room table undergoing, not only removal of the tumor itself, but also a foot of her intestines, and all her reproductive organs. We all had faith, however, that she would pull through it. Grampy, actually was the one who said it best that day in the hospital corridor, as he told his grandson, Scotty, "If there's anyone who can take the pain, it's your Nana. She's a fighter." Minutes became hours. Grampy, the Rush children, their wives, and grandchildren awaited word on her status in the family waiting room, anxiously biting nails and staring nervously into frozen space and time for the doctor to deliver the news of her outcome.

Finally, the surgeon emerged and said that he thought he got it all, but that we would all talk later about the need for her to undergo radiation or chemotherapy.

Marion, you see, ended up with a colostomy. In plain English, that meant that she would now go to the bathroom for #2 in a bag through an opening that emerged from the outside of her abdomen. At any rate, however, we could see her now.

And, what did this saint of a woman say when she awakened to all of her family staring and holding her hand in the recovery room? Trust me, it had nothing to do with herself, her pain, the embarrassment of knowing she had a bag on the side of her, or even her diagnosis. In typical fashion, this unselfish woman's only thought was that of her beloved husband.

"Did Grampy remember to take his pills?" she mumbled in an anesthetized stupor.

We answered her, astonished that she never asked a single question about herself, the operation, and in disbelief of the fact that she never shed a tear.

That was just the beginning of her fight with this demon, however. Upon her return home, she had to undergo 19 radiation treatments on an outpatient basis. (They call them treatments, but that's the nice word for them. In reality, they were 19 appointments that, towards the end, caused her abdomen to burn with the heat of a thousand suns, and for nausea and vomiting to become daily, unwelcome visitors in her home.) The colostomy caused her to have to go to the bathroom through a bag, washing it out each time, even when feeling frail and ill. Marion's daughter-in-law, Kathy, who lived downstairs, was a huge help in this regard, cleaning up at times when the bag would break and its contents would spill, soiling her mother-in-law's clothing, or when the stump on the outside of her stomach needed a dressing change, as well. It was enough for any person to lose themselves, their spirit, and their will to survive, but not our Nana.

Through it all, however, Marion remained upbeat and happily conversant with all the medical professionals and family members she encountered. She shopped for a wig with her sisters, Avis and Ruthie, thinking she would lose her hair. (Thankfully, she never did. She considered herself lucky for that. Imagine … lucky is what she thought she was?) And, she never, ever lost her will to live. She never gave up.

Six months later, after all those excruciating treatments and the many plastic bag changes that goes along with the embarrassment of having to go to the bathroom through a hole in your side, she received word from the surgeon on her case that she would have to undergo yet another operation. At least this time, there was an "up-side" to the news. She would undergo what they call a colostomy reversal. This meant that she would be able to relieve herself in the normal, accepted fashion. She would be able to become whole again, losing the hole in the place where it didn't belong.

Thankfully, that operation was a success, except for a minor glitch the doctors called an ileus. It was explained that this is the medical equivalent of a stunted bowel, which ultimately caused her to have to return to the hospital's Cummings Rehabilitation Unit. The physical and occupational therapy she received there, along with the wonderful nursing staff helped solve this problem, and get her back on her feet. A few weeks later, Marion returned back to her Granite Street home. She had fought—and beaten—the ugly C-word-monster that insidiously burrowed within her. The glory of her fighting spirit prevailed, and the sparkle in her big brown eyes returned. She, like the proud athlete she once was, hit a homerun out of the ballpark.

The only trouble was that another opponent was on deck ready to throw her yet another curve ball, only, this time, it was coming from high and inside.

22

The Heart of Glory

Healthwise, one might say, Nana and Grampy remained pretty much on an even keel for a few years after Marion's battle with colon cancer, staying afloat of any major problems with the help of family members bringing food to them, helping them with household chores, and, in the months of May and September each year (when their daughter Pat and her husband Richard would come to visit), taking them for boat rides on Lake Winnepesaukee in New Hampshire to visit Marion's sister, Avis, and her husband, Don.

When Avis and Don first purchased their condominium at Weir's Beach, New Hampshire, the whole family would gather for her famous cookouts, even Gracie was there, as her daughter, Donna, also owned a condo near the lake and a pontoon boat, to boot! The whole Rush family was treated to lazy boat rides on the lake, frequently stopping at the arcades to play the pinball machines, skee-ball, or Bingo at nightfall. It was fun for all, even Nana and Grampy, now in their mid-80s, who good-naturedly stayed the weekend in a modest cottage on the lake's Christmas Island to be with their daughter and the other relatives for the family reunions.

Yes, it was true: the waters were calm for several years. Abruptly, however, a wave of bad news from the medical world rocked the boat, once again, for Marion just when she thought she was sailing along on borrowed time.

No one in the family seems to remember if it was a single event that resulted in her diagnosis of CHF ... we all just know it has been the one opponent that came from high and inside her chest that has been—and remains to this day—to take its toll and wreak havoc on Marion's embattled, bony body.

CHF stands for congestive heart failure, resulting (in Marion's case) from a leaking heart valve. Dr. Berg discovered Marion to have this affliction after she continued to have frequent episodes of shortness of breath with fatigue and dizziness. The option was presented to her to be operated on to repair the leaking valve that was causing blood flow and fluid to back-up around the heart (and in some instances, the lungs) OR to have her condition managed through medication, specifically the anti-diuretic drug, Lasix, which helps rid the body of the excess fluid.

Marion chose the latter treatment: the Lasix, and it has been a decade-long delicate balance of dosage administration, weight management/scale watching, and hospitalization after hospitalization followed by rehab stint after each at the Cummings Rehab Unit for resultant complications ever since the decision was made to manage the CHF in this manner. (Of course, an operation to repair the leaking valve could have had the same consequences as well—or worse—but at least going this route didn't require open-heart surgery on an elderly woman in her mid-80s.)

(Coincidentally, Marion's sister-in-law Gracie, suffered from CHF as well. In fact, Gracie sadly passed away a few short years after Marion received the news that she, too, had the same condition. Also, several years before Gracie's passing, Marion's other sister, Ruthie, (the one who used to "steal" her nylons) was diagnosed sadly with lung cancer that later metastasized to her brain. This was another devastating blow to Marion, as she was also very close with Ruthie and her husband, Arthur—the ones who would go for drives with them to racetracks and Bingo "way up in New Hampshire.")

Which brings me to another complication that resulted from the CHF diagnosis: the loss of both Nana and Grampy's driver's licenses. With the CHF, Nana could pass out behind the wheel and Grampy ... well, he had lost too much reaction time due to age and dementia settling in to his near 90-year-old brain. Dr. Berg had to break the news to them that it was time to retire the Rush-red Oldsmobile, as Jimmie and Marion (with their combined heart and health issues) were just too much of a risk to themselves—and to others—to be on the road. It was devastating news to two independent people whose idea of fun was to get in the car and go for short excursions and Sunday rides up to New Hampshire or to the nearest dollar store or fast-food restaurant.

It was also difficult on the family, particularly their son, Jimmie Jr. and his wife, Kathy, their primary caregivers, who then became in charge of watching Marion's salt intake (due to the CHF), administering medication, weighing her in, and going to countless doctor's appointments. (Marion's other son, Eddie, my husband, would oftentimes be called upon to help out in this regard, particularly with literally carrying his mother up and down the full flight of stairs of their Granite Street home with his brother, as she did not have the strength to do so on her own accord.)

Just when the family settled in to some semblance of acceptance of Marion's CHF and its lifestyle consequences on everyone involved, another health issue emerged. It was the morning of Easter Sunday, 2004, and Marion's son, Eddie, received a phone call from his brother, Jim. Their mother had to be rushed to Melrose-Wakefield Hospital yet again. She was having abdominal pains with subsequent vomiting. (It was very difficult to watch the agony she went through in the ER, as poor Marion was so sickly. We would wipe her mouth, only to have her vomit time and time again. After several hours in the ER, and after completion of an abdominal CAT scan, it was determined that she had a hernia and would need yet another operation.

So, once again, Marion underwent abdominal surgery followed by, yet again, another stay on the 5th floor of Melrose-Wakefield's Cummings Rehabilitation Unit. (Upon her return home, Kathy had to nurse the wound back with a belly-banded girdle, as Marion developed a hematoma (blood tumor) that took several weeks to heal.

Still, despite this and all Marion's other problems, she would continue to do what she could for her husband, herself, and her family, because she never wants to bother or be a burden to anyone. Despite her fatigue and shortness of breath over the next several years, she continued to dress herself, bathe herself (and Grampy, before it got to be too much), and help dress her elderly husband (oftentimes getting out of breath bending over to put *his* socks and shoes on, even though he was capable of doing so himself). Yet, she continued to bake several lemon meringue pies to send to relatives houses on holidays, cook up batches of brownies, make meals for herself and her husband, and crotchet afghans, sweater-sets, and mittens for all the newborn babies in the family—all while being Red Sox Nation's #1 fan, watching every game, score, and reading about every player's life, as well as doing the same for the New England Patriots and any other televised college baseball, football, or basketball team. If she wasn't busy doing these things, Marion could be found sitting on their front porch watching any Little League games playing across the street. When family members would come to visit, her face and big brown eyes sparkled, especially if they brought her lottery or scratch tickets for her to take a chance on lady luck.

One day, however, her luck ran out.

It was the day that changed the way she viewed her life, and the day she decided it was time to write a book about it.

23

The Glory in the Big Bang Theory

She fell with a thud out of the blue—didn't even feel it coming, she just dropped like a hard ball on the hardwood of the dining room floor of the second-floor apartment she shares with her husband of 64 years. And, she broke it—her right arm, that is. The arm, that in those glory days of 1939–43 fired smokin' hot fastballs back to the plate at the famous Boston Garden where she was known as Schulzie, first "baseman" for the professional women's softball team, *The Boston Olympets.*

She is up at bat one more time. It is her turn to turn the tide in the game. "Schulzie! Schulzie", her teammates scream from the bench. Then she hears her now-deceased brother, Al's, voice shouting his pet name for her from the stands of heaven, "Go get 'em Wo-Wo!" (He always called her that because of her charmingly enthusiastic way of saying 'Whoaaaaaa!' whenever excited.) She hears his chant loud and clear: "Go. Go. Wo-Wo!" And, hearing his voice again, she jolts back to reality, and snaps back to consciousness.

Meanwhile, downstairs, Jim, Kathy, Kelly, and Kara hear *"The Big Bang"* and come rushing upstairs to find Nana on the floor, dazed and confused as to how in the world she got there. Yet, somehow this now elderly athlete finds her inner strength; she rallies, albeit shakily so, and rises to her feet. A ride to the Melrose-Wakefield Hospital ensues and Marion, once again, becomes a patient lying on a gurney in the emergency room in an open-ended johnny—a number in the healthcare deli line—waiting her painstakingly slow turn in ER eternity to be seen by a doctor to be wheeled off to wait, yet again, for x-rays in the radiology department.

The calls to the family go out to be by her side.

Unbelievably, she is discharged back to home with an appointment the next week to see an orthopedic surgeon. He determines that in order to fix her broken shoulder, she will need, of all things: a *Rush* rod. The doctor explains that if she does not have this operation, her right arm, her throwing arm, her everything arm, will be as useless as an empty floppy sleeve.

She concedes to undergo the operation at the age of 89. It is a success! Yet, Marion needs to go for more rehab, once again, in the Cummings Rehabilitation Unit. She works so hard in her physical and occupational therapy that the therapists admire, respect, and adore her. (Some of them even remember her from her previous admissions.) When her nurses (notably Lillian) ask her about her past, Dr. Berg (who was writing in her chart on the unit) pipes up.

"Tell them, Marion, about how you used to play ball."

"Well,"says Lillian, "you should write a book. I would be the first to buy it!"

But, Marion, seems to let that thought go to the back of her mind, as her eyes begin to lose their sparkle and the pain from the injury and the countless subsequent physical therapy sessions take over. She asks to go back to her room to rest her weary and injured bony arm and body. All the PT and OT sessions are taking its toll, and she wonders if she will she be able to return home. The trauma of the fall is affecting her future outlook.

That same afternoon, while taking her nap, she awakens to the lovely face of her granddaughter, Lauren, who just happened to bring along another friend of the New Hampshire Rushes, Fr. Paul Gilbert, a young priest from Manchester, New Hampshire, whom both Marion and her husband absolutely adore. She slowly opens her big, brown eyes.

"Oh, my Glory! Fr. Paul!" exclaims Marion. After the exchange of a few pleasantries, he asks her if she would like to receive the Sacrament of the Sick. She is enthusiastic at this prospect, yet somewhat reticent, knowing that this ritual used to be called by Catholics years ago as: The Last Rites. At one time it was known as the end-of-life sacrament, the one that priests would administer only to those individuals who were sickly enough to be knocking on heaven's door. He slowly takes out a vessel filled with Holy Oil, that he keeps in his vestment pocket and anoints her on the forehead: "In the name of the Father, the Son, and the Holy Spirit." He continues with his prayer, and then resumes talking with Marion about other things such as their mutual love and respect for their favorite baseball team: The Boston Red Sox.

Later that evening, long after Fr. Paul's visit, a change comes over Marion. She seems, to the family, revitalized with a new enthusiasm, and the twinkle in her softened, brown eyes returns. She is talkative to the point of a desert-dry mouth. The family becomes concerned that the medication she is taking is having some side effects on her personality. She seems consumed and obsessed with the prospect of writing the biography of her life, and that is all she wants to talk about with them. Happiness is apparent all over her glowing, radiant countenance. She credits Fr. Paul and the sacrament he performed with this miracle. She feels, she tells us, like a new woman, energized and enthused. From that moment on, and, for the rest of her rehabilitation stay, Marion is fixated on her biography/memoir. She can't sleep. All she thinks of is "Da Book," or "the darn book," as she calls it. When Eddie, her son, and myself visit one night, she asks me the question pressing on her mind: "Would I write this book for her?" I answer her, equally as enthusiastic and humbled by her offer, for I am delighted to have been offered this opportunity to do so for the incredibly beautiful, sweet-souled and wonderful woman that my mother-in-law is.

Since then, she has dictated (and I, with my husband, Eddie's help, have transcribed and authored) her memories, notes, and "Nanaisms" on this most beautiful and unselfish woman. She is my inspiration, our family's matriarch, and a saintly sweetheart of a person.

She is now 90-years-old and her story continues to this day, of course, with her family forever by her side as she encounters and endures more health-related episodes. But, like the true athlete she was and is, she perseveres for the team, "the club," the family.

24

It Takes a 'Glory-ous' Village (and better yet—good insurance)

It isn't the glory and fame of the *Olympets* legacy with its numerous newspaper articles, impressive stats, and pictures of herself in print that matter most to Marion. Though that was a golden moment in that time of her life, it isn't, by any stretch of the imagination, her proudest accomplishment. Even the triumphant accolades she received as a Malden High School all-star or her athletic prowess as a member of the Melly and Collins' Club don't even come close to what she considers the crowning glory of her 90-years. In fact, the thing that makes Marion's softball-sized brown eyes smile the most has nothing at all to do with her athletic achievements. The starting lineup she is the most proud and happy to be a member of is the one that doesn't have a snapshot mentality that cares for her because of some past glory-filled moments. The team Marion cares most to be on—and is the most proud of is—her family. She, instead, relishes and basks in the glory of each individual's accomplishments with unbridled enthusiasm and a few gusto-enhanced: "Whoa, oh my Glory's!" Family is what Marion is all about. She believes with all her heart that it is the only club or team in life that really matters: the one she gave up glory and fame for way back when. She knows that they aren't just a bunch of players on a softball diamond who disband at the end of the season. Family is defined as the people who are there for you in summer, winter, spring, and fall, to catch you throughout all the hard knocks in life (like the time she literally was knocked to the floor and broke her shoulder). They are the group of members she knows that love her not because she threw a ball or used to hit one better, faster, or farther than another woman on a softball diamond. Her family loves her because she is a diamond of a woman: humble, positive, pure and kind—and for that she shines brighter than any present-day-athlete's star.

Of course, by the term family, Marion means just about anyone and everyone who befriends her. People want to be in her inner circle because she is who she is:

an absolute sweetheart of a woman. Within the "village" of Malden and beyond, she has many family members, not only her obvious loved ones like her husband (Jimmie), sons (Jim and Eddie), daughter (Pat), daughters-in-law (Kathy and Denise), son-in-law (Richard), granddaughters (Kelly, Kara, and Lauren), grandson (Scott), sister (Avis), brother (Arthur, a.k.a. Junie), brother-in-law (Avis' husband, Don), but her "family" extends beyond that to include nieces (namely, Ruthie's daughter (Cathy, and her husband, Kenny), Gracie's daughter (Donna, who continues to visit her weekly), as well as her sons (Alan and Billy) and their wives (Heather and Roberta), who also bring their children to cheer up Marion on occasion, and for whom she has knitted many of the aforementioned outfits that have kept her hands busy in the retirement years. Then, of course, there are the other people who have recently cared for her as she has aged, whom she also cares deeply about, such as her beloved physician (Dr. Berg), her hairdresser (Donna), a friend of the family (Jamie, a young nurse), her caretakers hired by Jim and Kathy to help them out with Nana and Grampy's care as they entered their 90+ years (Judy, Laurie, and Lucy), and also any nurse assigned to the Melrose-Wakefield Hospital, as well as those stationed on the Cummings Rehab Unit, and, of course, most notably, Fr. Paul Gilbert, the young priest and friend of the Rush family, who lovingly visits Jimmie and Marion and brings them spiritual and moral support during times of sickness and subsequent hospitalizations.

Indeed, all these individuals comprise the "village team" of people who have done everything in their power to keep both she and Grampy healthy, independent, and out of a nursing home. Each has used their time and talents to help in that regard. Of course, at times, there has been a cost. For Jim and Kathy (the primary caretakers), and their daughters, Kelly and Kara, it has taken a toll on their family. They have been called upstairs in the middle of the night when they have heard Marion or Jimmie fall down. (Once, Grampy had a seizure, and it was Kathy who rubbed his chest till he "came-to" on the floor. This episode led to a hospitalization for Grampy at the Beth Israel Hospital, where good ol' Fr. Paul, their family friend, administered to Grampy the sacrament of the sick.) Jim and Kathy have also been called to come home from a vacation in Disney World, Florida. Kelly has devoted much of her 20-something life to the care of her frail, edentulous, Grampy, grinding his food, putting him to bed, and, as Grampy would say, "what have 'ya." Kara has done their laundry. Son, Jim Jr., has had to change his father's soiled underwear that, at times, were found mysteriously hidden in dark corners of the house, as Grampy was too embarrassed at his "accidents."

So, too, has the effort to keep his parents safe and out of harm's way, free from the grip of disease, taken its toll on their other son (Eddie) and his family who live in New Hampshire. For years, he, along with myself, and frequently our children (Lauren and Scott) would make Friday night or Saturday morning trips to visit his parents so that Eddie could give his father his weekly shower. (Lauren, who works in the healthcare field, comforted Nana greatly in her decision to go to the hospital the day before Christmas when she had a bad case of bronchitis.) Scott, her only grandson, would call frequently and visit from college, even with his friends, to bring joy to his Nana's day.) Our family also brought meals, on occasion cooked for them, and visited with them at home or whenever either Nana or Grampy were hospitalized. Throughout his parents' later years, Eddie received innumerable calls at work, having to leave his job on countless occasions to literally help carry his mother down the stairs to take she and his father to medical appointments. Our family has also been right by Nana and Grampy's bedside (along with the downstairs Rushes) during those trying times as well, whether it was Easter Sunday or Christmas Eve, as was the case on two of Nana's emergency room encounters.

Of course, helping out with their care was harder for their daughter, Pat (and her husband Richard) as they live in Florida. But, when they did visit, they did their best to share responsibility, taking Grampy out for rides, making candy with her mother, playing Scrabble and other board games with Nana, and, for Richard, installing bathroom safety equipment, walker-wheels or performing any other handyman projects around the house.

Marion's niece, Donna (and, at times, her husband, Bill) would visit "Auntie Marion" weekly, without fail, whether Marion was at home or in the hospital. Nana's niece, Cathy (Ruthie's daughter), would visit and also cut Grampy's hair to help out. Her husband, Kenny (who has polio with a resultant asymmetric leg) also did his part, as he would take Grampy out for rides while Nana stayed home, as she could not go up and down the flight of stairs in the house due to her CHF. Brother, Junie, checked in on her whenever he came to Malden from his second home in Florida. He also wrote faithfully to his sister on a weekly basis. Marion's sister, Avis, and her husband, Don, once stayed an entire week downstairs in Jim and Kathy's apartment caring for Marion and Jimmie, so that Jim and his family could take a respite vacation at their Disney World timeshare. (For years, they have slept with two baby monitors by their bedside, having to listen for any thuds in the night or calls for help from upstairs.) Donna's sons, Alan and Billy, have also visited their "Auntie Marion" with their wives and children on many weekends, their babies bringing joy, sparkle, and twinkle to the forefront of Marion's big, brown eyes.

However, those aged eyes that had once either caught or dodged furious fastballs, could not foresee what was eventually coming their way—the need for nursing care beyond what this wonderful family and "village team" of caretakers could provide.

This time, the fall happened in the middle of the day. It was during the time lapse when the caretakers, Judy and Laurie, were off their "shift" and Jim and Kathy were not yet home from work. Nana had her walker, her "chariot" as she calls it, the kind with the little seat between the bars. She was reaching in the refrigerator to get something when suddenly, she went down, yet again with a thud, and fell right on her tailbone, or coccyx, to use the medical term. She rallied, of course, in typical Marion Rush fashion, and got herself up. She never even realized that the fall was that bad. For the next couple of days, she had the heating pad on her behind, and, later, alternated that treatment with ice on a doughnut (and I don't mean the kind that comes from Dunkin's).

Well, about a week later, she yelled for Jim and Kathy to come upstairs. She could not get herself out of bed. Even though she was pulling on her bedrail with all the might her stick-figured arms could muster from her 86-pound, bony-bruised body, she just could not gather the strength, and the pain was excruciating. It wasn't hard to figure out that she had to go to the Melrose-Wakefield Hospital—again.

After a three-week hospital stay, with two of them being spent yet again at the Cummings Rehab, the doctors determined (after she endured x-rays, CT, bone scan, and weeks of physical and occupational therapy) that Marion had sustained a fractured tailbone. Her pain was unbearable, especially when she needed to sit on the hard commode in her room or when she needed to sit up from a lying down position. It took the family to advocate for her. Thankfully, the order was written for the medicine most likely to alleviate her pain.

Through it all, she never cried, because she lives by the credo of the Tom Hanks' line in the movie *A League of Their Own,* "There's no crying in baseball." And life, in Marion's eyes, is always about baseball. Actually, she only welled up at one point. It was during a therapy session with her physical therapist, Chris. Marion was actually her star pupil in PT. But, one day, Marion overdid it. As usual, she pushed herself too hard doing leg exercises while sitting on, of all things, a big ball—a medicine ball—they call it. As we understood it, with the PT holding her, she had to catch and throw other balls from that vantage point. (A feat that the old, younger Marion could perform with her eyes closed.) The next day, she was in excruciating pain. Add to that stress, the fact that she knew the Cummings Rehab Unit was closing forever … finito. In the next two weeks, Marion's safety net at the Melrose-Wakefield would no longer exist. She knew she had to work harder than ever if she wanted to return home. However, she also understood she was just in too much pain and too weak and wobbly from the CHF to return there, even with her trusty chariot alongside her. The reality of that hit home with her and those sweet brown eyes began to moisten. All along, her concern was not for herself, but for her husband, "What will happen to Grampy?"

It didn't take long for her positive outlook to resurrect, never becoming confused and always with all her faculties intact, including her sweet sense of humor. The next day, with her pain under control from a Lidocaine patch ordered by a consulting physician, she then persevered to become the Cummings Rehab MVP (most valuable patient.) She excelled in her leg lifts, she caught all the balls thrown to her in PT, OT was a breeze, and she went for walks with her new PT-approved "chariot" in the hospital corridors that she nicknamed "Main Street" with a right turn onto "Broadway." She characteristically put the positive spin on everything, telling her family her stay was like being in a hotel, calling down to room-service for meals and enjoying watching late-night Red Sox playoff games or Celtics basketball, along with any other televised sports. If her roommates were upset by the sound, she'd watch it with that off, just to get the scores. She'd plug her ears into her little radio at the same time, and she was lulled to sleep by the chatter of an ESPN or WEEI's sportscaster's voice. It's all music to Marion's ears.

What wasn't music, however, was hearing the news that she had to be moved to a nursing home for a short-term 30-day stay. That was all her insurance would allow. After that time-span, she would have to be reevaluated. She didn't have Medicaid, only an HMO, and that made the difference. Our society's laws said she would have to be private-pay until there was absolutely no money left in her account before she would be considered eligible to go on the state-funded program. She had to lose her life's savings. But, what would happen to her husband, Jimmie (a.k.a. Grampy) or as she affectionately calls him, "the Father."

That would be a bit of a problem. Though Grampy has dementia and was on the anti-seizure medicine, Neurontin, for it, he still had enough wits about him to know who his family is and to definitely know that he likes his home. But, sitting alone looking out the window, without "Mother" as he refers to his wife, was pretty lonely. The discussion about what do with Grampy, however, needed to take place.

Grampy shuffled into Nana's hospital room with Eddie and myself to visit his 90-year-old bride. They took him to the "aquarium" as Nana called it, also known as the solarium. There, they sat together on the loveseat, like the two wide-eyed, young and in love sweethearts they once were.

Marion grabbed her husband and once-upon-a-time boyfriend's hand and stared him straight into his baby-blue eyes. "Grampy," she said, "Would you be willing to stay overnight with me when I go to the nursing home? And, if you like it, will you come and stay with me?" The silver-haired 94-year-old and hard-of-hearing, Jimmie Rush, gazed into his sweetheart's big brown eyes. "Mother," he said in his characteristically low and shaky voice, "I'd follow you to the ends of the earth."

"That's what I wanted to hear," said Marion.

And, they kissed.

Six days later (after her sons and their wives checked out several nursing homes) Marion was admitted to the Annemark Nursing Home and Rehabilitation Center in Revere, MA.

When she learned they had Bingo, bowling, outings, and games to play, she was ecstatic. "I'm moving to a new condo," she joked. She was actually happy to be going to a nursing home. (How many people have an attitude like that?) Only, Marion Rush would. She's even willing and happy to stay there longer than those 30 days, if need be. She even said she realizes she can't go home. (A smarter woman there is not.) "If I go home, she said, I might fall again and have to start all over, perhaps ending up somewhere else." Of course, whether Grampy keeps his promise to meet his mate there and live with her in the same nursing home room remains to be seen. The family and the "village team" are there for him, as well, until that day comes. (We hope he does join her there, however, to honor and repay her, if you will, for all the deeds she has done for him over the years: ironing his clothes, cooking his meals, washing his clothes, combing his hair, dressing him, cutting his nails, and doing everything a wife could do—and more. All this is equally true of her care for him in his younger years, as well as in their golden years.)

Marion, the true team player, however, made a decision: she was going to enjoy her new nursing-home life. She's one of the few residents there with a cell phone in her pocket, and her ears (being the true member of Red Sox nation that she is) plugged in with her headphones into her little black radio. Of course, the TV is tuned to the sports channel, as well. That's our Nana!

She is truly one-in-a million. Marion now has her eyes set to earn a new title: MVP nursing home patient!

She has made her peace with what has happened to her and is ready to move on. In fact, when she saw the activity calendar at the Annemark that her son, Eddie, brought to her, she exclaimed, "Whoa, I think I'll be in heaven before heaven!"

Of course, typically, she has also made her peace with that place as well. Several months before the fall that literally landed her a way to "steal a new home," albeit a nursing home, she made some plans for her next one, instructing her daughter-in-law, Kathy, to do her a special favor. For years, Veronica Rush's name was not listed on the gravestone where she was buried with her father-in-law. Marion decided the time had come to forgive the woman who, for years, seemed to dislike her so much. She then paid the price to, at long-last, honor Veronica by adding and engraving her name to the tombstone of her mother-in-law's resting place.

She also did the same for herself and Grampy, instructing Kathy to make all her and Grampy's final arrangements. They will be buried side-by-side at the Puritan Lawn Cemetery in Peabody, Massachusetts, where her mother, Edie Mae, and her beloved father, Arthur Schulze, also lie in peace. It is a unique place, actually, with no headstones in the entire cemetery, just lush emerald lawn in the spring and summer months as far as the eye can see. In fact, the billboard on the Route 1 highway instructs visitors how to get there. It reads, "Visit the Park."

Marion Schulze Rush will like that just fine: a park to spend eternity. And, just like her early, Eastern Avenue cow-pasture-playing-days of yore with her brothers Al, Frank, and Junie, she will be forever happy on a little patch of green.

"Oh, *my* Glory!" That's my mother-in-law—a woman *In A League of **Her** Own.*

25

Just a Few 'Glory-ous' Nanaisms

The following are just a few of the sweet, cute, and sometimes funny 'Nanaisms' (as the family calls them) that make Marion the adorable, indelible, endearing character she is. These are not meant to belittle or make fun of her in any way, shape, or form. Rather, they are a way to convey a small portion of what makes our Nana, "our lovable Nana," a means to share and reveal to others the female Norm Crosby persona that lies within this sweetheart of a woman's personality. (They are in no particular order with the Nanaisms bolded within sentences):

- "Ooooooh, look at those kids in that yard, they're jumping on one of those **tambourines**." (Think she meant *trampoline*?)

- "My granddaughter works at that Dana **Farmer** Cancer Hospital." (It's really Dana *Farber* Cancer Institute.)

- "How 'bout that Dice-K Matzu-**ca-ca**?." (Nana really was referring to the million-dollar Japanese Red Sox pitcher, Dice-K Matsu*zaka*.)

- "I've got to have one of those, what-cha-call-it **Bavarian** enemas." (She really meant a *barium* enema, one of the tests she had during her many hospitalizations.)

- "Your Uncle Mac has to have something on his skin removed. He's going to have to see a dermatologist and have an **autopsy**." (Nana, really had us going on this one. What she meant to say was a *biopsy*.)

- "Let's go to the **aquarium** to sit down at the end of the hall." (As mentioned, it was the *solarium*.)

- "That Red Sox player was on that late-night talk show, the David **Finnegan** show." (It was actually, the David Letterman show.)

- "That picture frame is falling apart, I need to get one of those **cellulite** ones." (What she meant to say was one of those acrylic frames.)

- "Did you see where that **Omar** who's running for President is going to be in New Hampshire this weekend with **Opera**." (Our sweet Nana was referring to Barack *Obama* meeting up with *Oprah* Winfrey.)

- On another occasion, before the NH primary, when talking with Nana about some of the 2008 Presidential hopefuls, she said: "I watched that **Huckleberry** tonight on TV give a speech for a half-an-hour, and I really like him. I think it's going to be between him and that **Rockabama**." (Of course, she meant Mike *Huckabee* and, again, Barack *Obama*.)

We love you, Nana!

Epilogue

Approximately a month after Marion entered the Annemark Nursing Home and Rehabilitation Center, her husband of 64-years, the 94-year-old, white-browed, silver fox, Jimmie Rush, a.k.a. "Grampy," a man who literally puts the gentle in the word *gentle*man, arrived at the decision to join his wife. He sums it up in his own inimitable style, leaning his little-over-90-pound frail and delicate body habitus into his listener's space. It is a charming gesture that he has done throughout his life to earn the trust that inevitably turns a friend into a confidante when he shares his whisper-soft secrets.

"You know," he says in his low, gravelly voice, "I woke up one morning and said to myself … 'what am I some kinda punk?' Here I am in my home and my wife is in a nursing home. I used to say … 'a nursing home is not for me—it's just not my bag.'" (I chuckle inside, thinking: Could it be that Grampy is really a 94-year-old hippie … it's not my bag … how cute is that?)

"I used to say, I'm not like these people, all slumped over in wheelchairs and all, but, now I realize I belong here too. I have to do the right thing for my wife. She needs me."

And, with that, the once-upon-a-time, young-and-in-love sweethearts, are together again until the gossamer wings of angels whisk them both away ever so gently to the clouds of heaven's gate and into the hands of God. Until that day, however, they continue to hold each other's hands: the ones that father-time has weathered and creased through hard work and playing hard … and, in the case of Marion, playing hard ball as a professional ballplayer, wife, and mother—the latter two being roles that she continues to perform. Yes, she and her husband still enjoy each other's company. They go to bingo together, take walks together with their dueling walkers or "chariots" down the long hallway (she getting out of breath and easily fatigued as her 86-pound body copes with her CHF diagnosis). They continue to watch sports on TV together, with Marion the assigned keeper of the clickers and the runner of the VCR and DVD player. (She manages changing channels with one hand while fielding the family calls on her cell phone with the other.) Marion, forever the doting wife and 'mother' to her husband continues to help him in any way she can. It is just what she does: she will always and forever look out for Grampy. She helps him get out of bed, sometimes pulling him up with her once broken-shouldered-arm. She mashes the potatoes down with her own fork on his tray of food when he says, 'Mother, mother,' and she presses the call button for him to receive bathroom assistance from the nurses in the middle of the night, she being awakened herself in the process by the incessant clanging of his bed alarm. As always, she is quite simply: there for him, whatever his needs or wants. Gone are the days when she would cut his toenails, comb his hair, help him get his shoes and socks on and assist him with getting dressed, helping him ease into his pants. She could never bear to watch him struggle on his own, as he inevitably would end up with two legs in one opening. It seemed no matter how hard it was for her to keep her frail, bony body balanced or how out of breath she would get from her CHF, she helped Grampy. Even now she, characteristically, continues to give freely of herself, as best she can, foregoing and subjugating her own needs and wants for the one she loves. It is her secret to happiness. It is what makes Marion genuine. It is the secret to her life and marriage.

Yes, Marion and Jimmie, after all these years, are still together and in love. They have settled-in quite nicely into yet another stage of their lives: nursing home life. They are on a new team now, where its members move much more gingerly, never sliding home, and never looking back with regret at the plays they didn't make. For some elderly, like Marion and Jimmie Rush, the transition is easier. They have family who visit them regularly. They still have each other, and they cherish that. The sign on the door to their room serves as testament to that fact. It reads: Honeymoon Suite.

A word from the author

I tried to make this biography as historically accurate as possible, using Marion's memories as my compass and guideline. In that regard, I have written about past relatives in the manner and chronicity as she remembers them. One discrepancy that was pointed out was that her grandmother, Sadie, actually passed away when Marion was an adult. However, in her dictation, Marion had said that Sadie met her demise when she was in junior high. It was, thus, recorded as such.

My mother-in-law is an absolute living doll and saint of a woman, and I only hope and pray that this biography/memoir will serve justice to her depiction (and may, in some small way, pay tribute to the "village team" of people who have cared for her and her husband in their later years). I am hopeful that the facts and characters in this work are portrayed accurately, truthfully, satisfactorily, and that they clearly come to life within the framework of this incredibly unselfish, kind, and giving woman's life's story.

To the members of the Schulze and Rush "teams" she will always be the true representation of the *real Madonna*: *our* Mother Mary, the Mother Marion, if you will, in the legacy of our family's ancestry until she, one day, joins the "team of the saints" on heavenly turf.

978-0-595-49459-0
0-595-49459-5

Printed in the United States
107499LV00003B/357/P